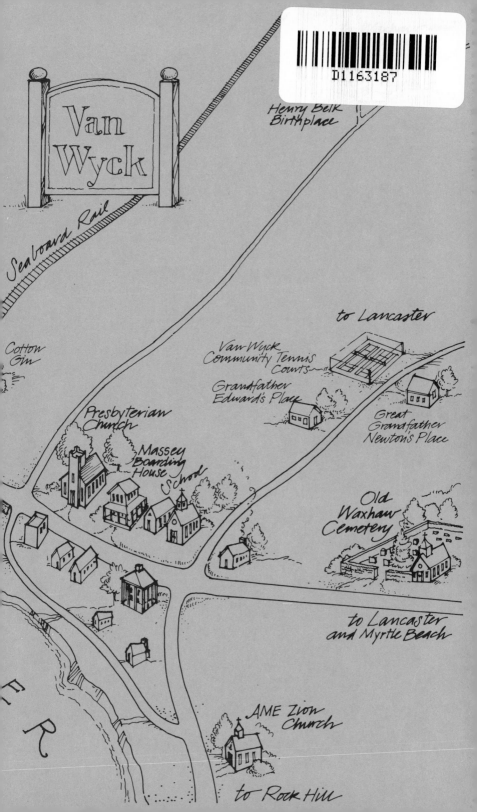

Boyhood On A Farm

Boyhood
On A Farm

James D. Nisbet

Books by James D. Nisbet

High Temperature Alloy Exploratory Research
The Entrepreneur
The Dow is Dead
Weathering Stock Market Storms
Boyhood On A Farm

GM PG JB BL

Published by
Capital Books
2900 14th St. North, Suite 45
Naples FL 33940
1-800-391-1161 or 941-263-1896

Libraries of Congress Cataloging-in-Publication Data............
Nisbet, James D
         Boyhood On A Farm.
         ISBN 0-9640139-1-6

IN MEMORY OF MY
MOTHER AND FATHER

ACKNOWLEDGMENTS

Many people contributed to writing this memoir. A special thanks to members of my family who were indispensable in helping me shape the book for publication. To my editors, sons Jim and Jack, who are real writers. To Claire, Jack's wife, and to Carol Hazard, my stepdaughter, who know their way around editing, writing and publishing. To Linda Winecoff, my artistic step daughter-in-law, who drew the map. To Robert Lee for beautifying an old black and white picture for the cover.

To Nancy Crockett, the aristocratic lady from the Old Waxhaws, who helped "on location."

And to James Robinson Nisbet, my distant cousin, and Catie and Charlie Cocke, for being cheerleaders when they read the first draft.

PREFACE

This book of stories is about the younger years of the boy on the left in the photograph on the front cover. On the right is his brother Oliver, sixteen months older and a little taller in 1920 when the picture was taken on a farm near the Catawba River in South Carolina.

The stories are about sharecroppers, neighbors, my family and a few relatives. About uncles who were uncles because they were kinfolks and about uncles who were uncles because they were old Negro folks who lived on our farm. A touch of the history of Van Wyck and Lancaster County, South Carolina, where I was born, is woven in.

Since stories don't usually happen in an orderly fashion, and since I don't remember the exact order in which they did happen, I will tell them at random, but still loosely tied to my age when I was growing up.

I left the South in 1937 and didn't return until twenty years later, except for brief vacations. In 1957, I started a new industrial plant in Monroe, North Carolina, not far from Van Wyck, to take advantage of the fact that Southerners are better workers because the vitamins in the Carolina vegetables are richer.

When I returned, I renewed my relationships with my family, and especially with Oliver, who joined me in my new company. I also renewed a casual acquaintanceship with Van Wyck, but I didn't realize how much my old home place meant to me until Oliver died in 1994. Then I was overwhelmed with the memories of my boyhood, and, for reasons I don't understand, I felt inspired to write down these stories of my youth. In a few short weeks, the stories flowed from my memory into this book.

E arly in 1887, a Seaboard Railroad passenger train, traveling on new tracks from Richmond to Atlanta, stopped to take on water for its thirsty steam locomotive. The water tower where it stopped was twenty five miles south of Charlotte, North Carolina, near a tiny settlement where Twelve Mile Creek runs into the Catawba River.

The train was pulling a private car with an officer of the Seaboard Railroad, General Hoke, and his wife aboard. Mrs. Hoke got out of the car to stretch her legs and look around. She asked the conductor the name of the place and he shrugged. "We just call it South Carolina #1, Ma'am. It's the first water tower south of the state line."

The lady observed a half dozen smoking beehive kilns at a brickyard on one side of the tracks, a large two–story brick store on the other side, and a few well–kept houses nearby.

Mrs. Hoke liked the village so much that she gave it her maiden name—Van Wyck. This is the same name that has been given to the Van Wyck Expressway in New York City. Today, everybody who travels will recognize that name as the passageway from downtown New York City to the rest of the world via LaGuardia and JFK.

Before the train pulled away, a section foreman, the first local railroad employee, climbed off. He was to reside in the village and take charge of maintenance on the forty miles of track from

1

twenty miles north at Monroe, North Carolina to twenty miles south at Chester, South Carolina.

The section foreman's first duty was to hire a carpenter and build a two–room depot. The foreman was also told to build a three–room house for himself on the railway's right–of–way across the road from the depot. In those days a three–room house could be built in a few weeks because it wasn't complicated by inside plumbing or electrical wiring or closets. The insides of the walls were covered with newspaper to keep out the cold winter wind. Windows were small, without glass panes or screens. They had to be opened during the day for light and closed at night against the elements and whatever critters lurked outside.

Blueprints and materials for both house and depot were in a boxcar that had been parked on the brickyard siding the day before. Also in the boxcar was a maintenance inventory of ten dozen crossties and 10,000 railroad spikes. There was a hand–pumped jitney and trailer for use by the foreman and his crew for traveling the forty–mile maintenance route.

By and by, the depot was built. It was painted yellow and a sign reading "Whites" was placed above one entrance to the depot; the door to the second room was labeled "Colored". At that time, segregated waiting rooms were a matter of course not only for private offices, and bus and train stations, but for all public buildings.

Two signs, one pointing north and one pointing south, identified the new station as Van Wyck, South Carolina—its first official designation. Family legend has it that my father, who was a young boy at the time, climbed on top of some boxes on the loading platform to watch the city fathers christen the depot and and its new name with a bottle of homemade blackberry wine. A second stamp of approval was put on the name on June 25, 1889, when the U. S. Government rented space for a post office from the Massey–Yoder Store. Mr. Charles S. Massey was appointed the first postmaster of Van Wyck. I wonder if politics were involved when the owner of the original store in Van Wyck could both rent space for a post office and get himself appointed postmaster.

Prior to the visit of the former Miss Van Wyck, the village had been generally referred to as Little Waxhaw, or Waxhaw Township, after the farming area known as the Old Waxhaws which spread east from the Catawba river and north across the state line into North Carolina.

The greatest claim to fame for the broader area of the Old Waxhaws was as the birthplace of two presidents of the United States. James K. Polk, the eleventh president, was born in the small village of Pineville, North Carolina, a few miles north of Van Wyck. The seventh president, Andrew Jackson, has his birthplace claimed by two nearby towns: Waxhaw, North Carolina and Lancaster, South Carolina, just across the state line from each other.

But long before there were presidents or post offices or railroads, or even state lines, the junction of Twelve Mile Creek with the Catawba River was a well–known place. This was the spot where generations of Catawba Indians had come to collect a rare blue clay from which they molded and fired fine pottery. By the time the railroad arrived, the Catawba Indians were living on a reservation west of the Catawba River. They had survived wars with other tribes and illnesses that had reduced their numbers from several thousand to a few hundred. The Old Waxhaw territory was named after the Waxhaw Indian Tribe that had camped on the east side of the Catawba River. As the Waxhaw Indians died from sickness, and wars with the Catawbas in the late 1600s and early 1700s, first and second generation English and Scotch–Irish Presbyterians began to move down from Pennsylvania and Virginia. They became landowners and slave owners and cotton plantation farmers until the Civil War ended that era.

After the long process of picking themselves up from the ruins left by the war, the next generation of men slowly reevaluated their resources of raw materials and industries. In the Carolinas, cotton planters who had shipped their bales to New

England for processing into sheets and socks started shipping the bales down the road a piece to local mills for processing into sheets, socks, pillowcases, and carpets and to local apparel sewing lofts.

While this was all happening during the last century, Mr. Bill Ashe saw the potential for establishing a brickyard in the corner between the Catawba River and Twelve Mile Creek to turn the rare bluish clay into hard red brick. The bricks were fired in beehive–shaped kilns, hand stoked with coal from West Virginia. Because of the uneven heat, the bricks baked into colors ranging from deep red to almost black, depending on the type of iron oxides formed at the different temperatures. The new railroad brought the coal from West Virginia and delivered brick to far–flung housing markets, and Mr. Ashe anticipated a thriving business.

So the little settlement of Van Wyck grew up alongside the kilns, its economy supported by a weekly payroll to brickyard workers, weekly advances by landowners to sharecroppers and hourly payments to tenant farmers, and the continuous buying power of the landowners themselves.

This positive cash flow was an invitation for new merchants to open new stores in the village. The visionary ones could see the beginnings of a trend for even more payrolls as the tenant farmers gradually started to take jobs in the textile mills and apparel lofts that were springing up in nearby towns.

I am not certain what it was that attracted my forebears to the area. I do know that my great, great, great, great grandfather warmed himself around Old Waxhaw fireplaces a long time ago. His headstone is one of the oldest to be found in the Old Waxhaw Church Cemetery, the historical centerpiece of the Old Waxhaws:

Here Alexander Nisbet {1731–1773} lies and his wife Agness likewise.

The epitaph goes on to name their six sons and two daughters. Those six sons and two daughters grew to produce their own prolific broods, but the countryside was never thick with Nisbets because many of them were restless and curious to find what lay beyond the banks of the creeks and rivers around Old Waxhaw.

If I have my ciphers right, my great–great–great–grandfather was Colonel William, my great great was William II, my great–grandfather was Dr. John Newton, my grandfather was Edward William and my dad was John Edwin. They all stayed. My great–grandfather, Dr. Newton Nisbet, practiced medicine in Van Wyck. He passed away at seventy–six, having lived long enough to see the first train travel through his medical domain.

My dad, John Edwin Nisbet, was seven years old when the Seaboard tracks were laid through Van Wyck. He lived with his parents on a farm a mile north of Van Wyck and it must have been quite a thrill for him to be awakened by the late night whistle from the powerful steam locomotives as the trains braked and stopped in Van Wyck to take on water and pick up a few fresh carloads of bricks or cotton. I bet Dad wanted to slip down to the brickyard and stow away before the very next train huffed and puffed away from the station and traveled to faraway places.

For a time, while trains came and went, Dad stayed put, living and working on my grandfather's farm. When he was fourteen and in the eighth grade, he told his father that he would rather be a full–time farm hand than to continue school. After the end of my father's first farm season, my grandfather gave him a bale of cotton, which Dad sold for enough money to buy his first bicycle. With the bicycle and the use of one of the farm horses, he extended his territory and became acquainted with merchants in Waxhaw and as far away as Monroe, North Carolina.

When he was seventeen years old, Dad announced to his father that he had gotten a job as clerk at the B.D. Heath Company store in Monroe for fifteen dollars per month and wanted to leave home. He took the new job and was so good with figures that he was soon promoted to office boy;

after three years, Mr. Heath offered to pay his way to a three–month business course at a school in Macon, Georgia.

Dad told the story to us this way: he turned down the offer and told Mr. Heath he would go to the Georgia business school but that he had saved enough to pay his own way. When he returned he would negotiate for a suitable salary before going back to work. Mr. Heath was taken aback but most favorably impressed by this young man and doubled his salary when he returned.

At the time, Dad's Uncle Jule was managing the farms that his mother, Jane Phifer Nisbet, had inherited from her husband, Dr. Newton Nisbet, Jule's father and Dad's grandfather. Uncle Jule was a laid–back bachelor farmer. He liked to hunt more than he liked to manage a large farm.

Uncle Jule, aware of Dad's success as a merchant, encouraged him to return to Van Wyck and open a store. Uncle Jule offered to give Dad all of his household and farm trade from the two thousand acres he managed. That, coupled with the same offer of trade from Dad's father, was enough encouragement to seriously consider putting up all his savings to build a store in Van Wyck.

At that time, around the turn of the century, there were already three stores in Van Wyck, all built next to each other on the same side of the street facing a wide brick sidewalk. The oldest store was constructed with brick made at the local brickyard. The two other stores were constructed of wood. If a shed roof had been built from each store over the sidewalk, then the place would have looked like an old western mining town. Actually that might have been appropriate, because gold had been panned from all the river branches and creeks in that area before and after the Civil War. The gold was minted into coins in the nearby Charlotte Mint, which operated until the late 1800s and closed after gold mining went west.

The Massey–Yoder store, next door to the depot, was the oldest and the largest. It occupied the only two–story building and carried an inventory of coffins on the second floor. The store sold burial insurance that included the selection of a coffin that could be put on layaway at the store until it was needed, or until its time arrived, so to speak.

Dad was in his early twenties when he decided that Van Wyck could support a fourth store. Using a mason named Huss Barber, Dad built a substantial brick building with a full basement. It had two large plate glass display windows in the front, but did not have the customary elevated cashier's station in the middle of the store for the owner to keep an eye on the clerks. My dad figured he could manage the cash with a countertop cash register while acting as chief clerk.

There was a local telephone system in Van Wyck in those ancient times and the switchboard was in his store. He was the day–only operator, connecting neighbor with neighbor, and he might have listened in just a little, but not very often. That telephone system was abandoned when Dad closed his store not long after the turn of the century and long before rural electrification, which didn't arrive in Van Wyck until 1935, along with F.D.R. and the New Deal. Phones didn't return until 1938.

A memorable mystery Dad told me about concerned his method for keeping his cash. There was a portable safe in his store, but Dad was afraid someone would break in at night and cart it off to be blown open later. His solution was to take the cash home every night for *safe* keeping, and of course everybody in town knew about it. Daddy lived about a mile and a half from the store with his father and stepmother, a testy lady we called cousin Ida. Dad would ride his horse to and from his store every day. On Saturday he stayed open late, and if there was no moon, it was pitch black by the time he locked up and mounted his horse for the short ride home. The horse knew the way with or without the moon and plodded along, sure step by sure step.

One moonless Saturday night on the trip home, the horse jerked abruptly and vigorously to one side. Dad was barely able to avoid being thrown as the horse took off at full speed and galloped all the way home. Dad never doubted that a thief, waiting by the side of the road, had grabbed for the horse's bridle and was ready to kill for the cash. Thereafter the horse remembered, and Dad was happy to let him briskly trot home on a dark night.

After a few years of storekeeping, my father became uncertain about his future. He was twenty–six years old, a bachelor, and was trying to decide whether he wanted to continue to operate his small store in Van Wyck and be another department store magnate like one of his contemporaries from the Old Waxhaws, Henry Belk, or be a dirt farmer and settle on the land that he would inherit. His store was a good living for a bachelor, but it would have to expand to support a family.

In 1906, at the same time Dad was considering a change, a smart young schoolteacher named Strauss Walker checked in at Miss Massey's boarding house next to the one–room country schoolhouse on the hill above town.

Miss Strauss, as she was called, had grown up in York, South Carolina. Her father was a doctor and believed that all four of his daughters should have a college education. Strauss decided she would become a schoolteacher, one of the few professions open to young women at the turn of the century.

She first went to Winthrop College, the girls' school in Rock Hill, only ten miles from her home in York, but she was extremely homesick. College was not her happiest time. For her junior year she transferred to Columbia College, another girls' school in the capital of South Carolina. Before finishing her senior year she got an offer to teach in a little hamlet where a curve in the dirt road crossed a bend in the railroad tracks—Van Wyck, South Carolina.

She arrived in Van Wyck late in the winter of 1906, a midyear replacement for the lady who had been teaching at the town's one-room school. Years later she wrote an account of her first day teaching:

> I found myself, aged nineteen, entering the one-room, low ceilinged, weather-beaten school house. The children, about forty of them ranging in age from six to eighteen, had already assembled. It was a bitter cold March day, and the room was a hodge-podge of noise and confusion. Outside the wind tore at the pine trees and rattled the small windows. There was no sign of a stove in which to build a fire. The little ones clung to their big sisters.
>
> "I'm cold," each was saying, "cold and want to go home."
>
> Around me circled big farm boys with waiting, expectant faces. Dear God what shall I do?
>
> Mustering all the courage I possessed and trying to make my ninety-five pounds of

avoirdupois look as commanding as possible, I said in my most pleasant voice, "Children, Children, please be seated and tell me what is wrong and how the building is heated?"

From scattered remarks, I gathered their story. "We ain't gonna have school until Miss Julie comes back." "That other teacher called us brats." "She said we smelled bad." "No ways can we stay here without a stove." "We're going home." "That other teacher fooled you. She wasn't sick. We made her leave. We don't want you here neither."

One of the older boys summed things up. "We had as well go home. The stove's hid and no use you looking for it."

"Really children, I am sorry." Which indeed I was, and knowing nothing else to say or do, I said, "Let's bow our heads and repeat the Lord's prayer." Never before or since have I said the words more slowly or more fervently. "Deliver us from evil..." said with a truly contrite and broken spirit.

The prayer over, the room was deadly still. The forty heads raised: blue, brown and gray eyes searched the very depth of my soul. Oh God don't let them see that I am town bred, educated ...and a fool.

I broke the stillness. "Boys and girls, I would be sorry to have to leave. You see, I love it here. I think it is beautiful. I want you to give me a chance. Try me just for one day."

Strong brown hands dragged the stove from under the building. The stove was reinstalled, a basket of light wood with chunks of oak and hickory was piled into it. A match was lighted. Soon the little stove was dancing with heat.

Miss Strauss finished the term, and the following year she was hired full time.

M r. Massey, the Van Wyck merchant, was also the village matchmaker. He told Miss Strauss soon after she arrived that young Ed Nisbet was the most eligible bachelor around. Frail young Strauss Walker was embarrassed when her fellow boarders, who were traveling drummers, teased her and giggled about the potential romance that Mr. Massey was promoting.

Miss Strauss would never set foot inside Mr. Ed's store. She would cross over to the far side of the dirt road where there was no sidewalk, with her heart fluttering and her head held high, to avoid a face–to–face meeting with the handsome Mr. Ed, who stood six feet tall in the doorway of his store with his bushy black hair falling forward across his high forehead. She was not close enough to see his quiet gray eyes, but his florid complexion and his stout build were evident from across the road.

Miss Strauss, as I am sure you have figured out, became my mother. She told me this much about her romantic introduction to Van Wyck, but never followed through with any details about the development of the romance that led to her marriage to Mr. Ed the next year.

To keep my Presbyterian Scotch–Irish stock pure, I should explain how Mother came to be named Strauss. Mother's Aunt Ida had married the only Jewish resident of York, South Carolina, a Mr. Henry Strauss. He owned a furniture store and was a respected businessman. The couple could not have children, and when Mother was born they asked her parents if they would name their daughter Strauss. They also wanted Mother to live with them, and she did a great deal of the time. The understanding, or at least the expectation, whether spoken or unspoken, was that she would be the heir to the Strauss fortune. Mother was called Strauss rather than by her first name, Alice. Later on, we all had to explain from time to time that we were Scotch–Irish and not of the Old Testament faith.

When I was a boy in Van Wyck, nobody would have thought to question Mother's first name. It was years later, and only after I had lived several years in Schenectady, New York, that I learned about the implications of the name Strauss and the presumed differences between races and faiths; black, white, Jewish, and Catholic, and that I was supposed to have some prejudices.

Mother's aunt died before Mr. Strauss. He remarried and left his fortune to his second wife, leaving Mother with only her unusual name for an inheritance.

In 1908, the Nisbet clan from the Old Waxhaws and the Walker clan from further east around the Broad River, all traveling the short distances by train, gathered in York, Mother's home town, to attend the wedding of Alice Strauss Walker and John Edwin Nisbet.

It was decision–making time for my dad. He closed his store and moved to the eight hundred acres he had recently bought from the estate of his grandfather, Dr. Newton Nisbet. That land was two miles up the River Road and on the other side of Twelve Mile Creek from Van Wyck. It was across the road from Uncle Jule's place, which was bordered by the Catawba River.

Dad's father died that same year, and as the oldest son he inherited another six hundred acres, and so he set about managing two farms.

For the first year after they were married, Mother continued to teach. She would either walk or ride her horse the two miles to and from school. She had her own saddle which she had brought with her from her home in York, a sidesaddle of course. A young lady could hardly straddle a horse on either an English or a western saddle leaving her legs to dangle down each side of her horse, for that would have allowed not only her ankles but also her legs to show.

When she wasn't teaching, Mother exercised her authority over her new home by claiming a suitable yard from the cotton field which was growing to the edge of the house. She installed boxwood shrubs next to the house and jonquils all the way from the house to the road. She planted pecan trees around the boundary of the front yard to keep the cotton from trespassing. She had Uncle Stump dig up little cedars in the woods and planted them out along the roadside. The back yard was reserved for an orchard and grape arbor and vegetable garden.

The first child arrived in 1909, a boy. He was named John Edwin after our father, and everyone called him John Ed. Dad was called Mr. Ed. The second child was also a boy, and he was named Miles, after Mother's father, Dr. Miles Walker. Dr. Miles (we called him Papa) came by train from York for the birth of John Ed and Miles, as he did for all six of Mother's children. He delivered each child, arriving with only his bedside manner and his black satchel, enlisting the aid of a black lady and two kettles of boiling water. He delivered the girls without fanfare and the boys without circumcision.

Young Miles was a puny child with a cleft palate. He could not nurse and was very difficult to feed. Today it is hard for me to fathom that Mother and Dad were able to take their young son for an operation at Johns Hopkins in Baltimore. Medical insurance wasn't needed in those days. I am sure that Mother's uncle, Dr. George Walker, a resident physician at Johns Hopkins, must have signed the chit. But despite their best efforts, little Miles continued to waste away and died a few months later.

John Ed was two years old when Miles died. Subsequently, Nancy (1913), Oliver (1915), myself (1917), and little sister Alice (1920) rounded out the family.

We grew, we fought, we ate well, we played, we laughed, we solemnly went to church and Sunday school. We were an energetic and curious bunch of happy and noisy kids. We were also a healthy bunch for the most part, which was a good thing, since the nearest practicing physician was Dr. Sam Ezell, a cousin of ours, whose office near Lancaster was fifteen miles away.

When there was sickness, the family involved would "send word" to Uncle Sam and he would always be there, like Federal Express, before ten o'clock the next day. Sending word was telling neighbors the doctor was needed and neighbors would tell neighbors who would tell merchants in Van Wyck who would tell other neighbors. Soon Uncle Sam would get the word as surely as though by telephone, although not as fast. He would drive in the next day, sometimes the same day, in his Model T Ford Coupe with his black satchel, ready to tend to the sick who had "sent word."

Quite often, when Uncle Sam was anywhere near our place, he would stop by and visit with Dad for an hour or two. Often, while he was there, someone would recognize his car and "bring word" that old man Pettus, or whoever, was ailing and more stops would be added to Dr. Sam's itinerary.

Sometimes there wasn't time to send for Uncle Sam. One afternoon when I was a little tyke, I climbed a pear tree in the back yard. I was pretty high when a branch gave way and I crashed to the ground. The impact knocked the breath out of me. My sister Nancy witnessed the fall and was certain I was dead. Mother was away, and Nancy rushed to get Aunt Mag, the wash woman. By the time Aunt Mag arrived I had recovered my breath but my arm was in terrible pain and I told her to go away and let me die.

Aunt Mag told Nancy to hop on her horse and gallop to Uncle Verner's as fast as she could. Uncle Verner was a doctor and lived a mile or so north of our place. He was the youngest of my father's uncles, and he had degrees in pharmacy and medicine and became an entrepreneur by establishing a small pharmaceutical company in St. Louis. He sold his company a few years later and temporarily retired back to Van Wyck. He had arrived home driving a rare Stanley Steamer automobile, built a house deep in the woods on the Catawba River, and for five years meditated, farmed a little, and read medical journals. He resisted getting involved with the local practice of medicine, but that did not deter Aunt Mag when she found me splayed on the ground. A doctor was needed and Aunt Mag thought Uncle Verner could read his books some other time.

Uncle Verner came almost immediately. Nancy had caught him as he was returning home from town and he didn't have to wait the normal half hour to fire up the boiler to make the car run. I can still hear the Stanley Steamer coming, hissing and blowing like a snake or a steam locomotive, but without the clickety click of wheels on rails.

He set my arm there in the front yard and it hurt like hell. Then he strapped it to a splint which he made on the spot with a cut–off broom handle screwed to a shingle. Every morning for four weeks I would come downstairs carrying the splint in my good hand for Mother to refit and replace and get my arm back in a sling. My arm has been sightly crooked ever since, but it works okay.

D r. Verner was said by my father's maiden sister, Aunt Loma, to be an atheist. Whether or not that was true we will never know, but he did have a way of adding fuel to the idea. Once at a family Thanksgiving dinner at Aunt Emma Lee's house in Rock Hill, Uncle Verner was asked by Aunt Emma Lee (who should have known better) to say grace. Uncle Verner bowed his head and said,

"V. Nisbet thanks J. Christ for dinner. Amen." I suspect that he was not trying to be sacreligious as much as he was trying to be funny, for he was well–known for his sense of humor. Someone once asked him how long his mother had served grits, then called mush, for breakfast. He replied, "Oh, I am not sure, but I distinctly remember we had them for breakfast the morning I was born."

When I wasn't falling out of pear trees, I was usually trying to keep up with my two older brothers, John Ed and Oliver. John Ed was older by seven years than I and a hunter and a fisherman par excellence. He was an independent boy. Before we had our swimming pond and before Mother even suspected that he could swim, he came home one day and told her that he had swum across the Catawba River and back.

Oliver was my closest companion when we were boys. John Ed was also a good companion but, you know how it is, he was older. Oliver and I did our share of fighting and engaged in sibling rivalries all our lives, and one of the common ways we had to challenge each other was to dare the other. I will never understand how we got in our most serious daring position, but it was a dilly. I was standing on Oliver's pocket knife and refused to move. He held an axe about two inches above my head and dared me not to move. I stood my ground and Oliver let go of the axe.

The axe cut a deep gash in the top of my head and blood streamed down my cheeks. Fortunately, Mother and Dad were immediately on the scene and determined that the gash had not penetrated my skull and they patched me up. The cut left a little ridge in the top of my head, but it isn't noticeable because my hairline hasn't receded far enough to expose the area. Not yet.

I hold many memories of good times with John Ed and Oliver squirrel hunting in the woods and rabbit and quail hunting in the fields. In the fall, hunting quail with John Ed's pointers was always a great adventure. He kept two bird dogs, and trained them from the time they were young pups to thoroughly traverse the land thirty or forty yards ahead of us, continously sniffing for birds. The lead dog was always called Old Blue. It was fascinating to watch them running and sniffing around, then see them simultaneously stop and point with their noses straight toward the strongest scent—tails straight out to the rear, the paw of one front foot held six inches off the ground. The only comparable picture is a statuesque blue heron standing in the edge of a lake, stalking its prey. The dogs would "hold the point" and not budge as we walked forward, raised our shotguns, and released the safeties. The quail seemed to know that at some time between the dog's point and our arrival, it was time to go. This is the moment of high drama in quail hunting, and no matter how many times I experienced it, I was always startled when the covey of birds took off in a bluster of noisy flight.

John Ed would drop his sights on a bird and fire his twelve gauge double–barreled shotgun, then in an instant shoot again. Two quail would fall to the ground. As the covey reached the edge of the woods, I would take aim with my 410–gauge shotgun and shoot. Frequently, I missed. By the time I got my composure, after being startled by the bluster, the covey was often beyond my range. The dogs would stand rigidly in place until John Ed said "retrieve". They would bound away and a minute later they would bring back John Ed's birds and occasionally one for me. The hunt would continue, with the dogs pointing the "singles" that had landed in the woods. Then we would move to another field, hoping for another covey before darkness fell.

John Ed always had a half dozen rabbit boxes set in the field and woods as well as steel traps concealed in the stream below the swimming pond. I would frequently go with him on his daily trips to check on the catch from the night before. There were always one or two rabbits staring up from the bottom of the boxes. He took the rabbits home to clean them and sold them to Kirk Yoder for twenty cents apiece. Mr. Kirk would take the rabbits along with almost anything else on his frequent delivery service to Charlotte, where he sold them to grocery store butcher shops.

The steel traps, set for fur–bearing animals like mink, possum, otter and muskrats, were not as productive as the rabbit boxes. Two catches a week were pretty good and frequently we found that a mink had got the best of us by leaving his gnawed–off leg in the trap. He was long gone to live his life on three legs rather than grace the coat of a Lady Astor. John Ed took the trapped animals and skinned them, then dried the pelts over a frame he had bought, adjustable to suit the shape of the animals. A good mink pelt would bring two or three dollars from the fur traders who would periodically call on the local trappers.

We also spent a good bit of time fishing from a boat on the Catawba River, with a shotgun kept close by in case a duck or a goose was flushed. One cold winter day, John Ed and I finished duck hunting from the boat. I was cold and weary and wanted to go home. When he paddled near the shore, I couldn't wait; I jumped from the boat toward shore, and of course, pushed the boat from under me and landed squarely in the river up to my neck. We were a mile from home and I was freezing stiff. Fortunately, John Ed was an Eagle Scout and always prepared. He had matches and we built a fire and I stood naked by the flames as we dried my clothes before heading for home. Mother never knew what had happened.

Mother was not a strong disciplinarian. I remember very few whippings she gave me. One reason there were so few is because she would say to me. "Go cut a willow branch, I will switch you for that." By the time I returned, at least half an hour later, dutifully carrying a willow branch and a big smile on my face, Mother would laugh with me.

Mother was tolerant, loving and understanding. Even when her growing children were old enough to know they should not wet the bed, Mother changed the sheets and never complained or fussed about it. She would say nothing if the child would say nothing. If the child expressed guilt, Mother would say: "Nature will soon give you a signal to wake up, so we won't worry about it. We'll just wait and let nature have its way." Similarly, when one of the boys had a wet dream, nothing was said.

Daddy was the disciplinarian in our household. When he began to unbuckle his belt or went for his shaving strop and called for one of us to "stand here," we knew our misdeed had crossed the line of acceptable behavior and punishment was in order: ten lashes with the belt or the strop.

The "stand here" command occurred fairly frequently, but its execution was often completely discombobulated when the English bulldog we called Lion was present. Lion didn't take kindly to the "big master" of the house whipping his "young masters" of the yard, namely Oliver and me. At the command of "stand here," Lion would take *his* stand between Dad and the offender and growl and bare his teeth.

Dad knew better than to proceed with the whipping until he had put Lion, and himself, out of harm's way. By then he had frequently cooled down and would let the infraction pass with only five lighter lashes before returning the strop to the shaving stand where its more sensible and appropriate use was to sharpen his straight razor.

Dad sometimes tended to micromanage too severely. For example, soft drinks were never kept in our ice box. And when I say ice box, I mean ice box. There was not a refrigerator in our house until after I left home.

Soft drinks were limited, rationed to one Coke a week for each child. Years later as I drank a second or a third, even a fourth scotch and soda in one evening, I often thought about that rule. But I will never forget the pleasure of the tangy taste of a single Coke, from the old six–ounce bottle of course, as it washed down a mouthful of sardines and saltine crackers in Mr. Thompson's store on a Saturday afternoon in Van Wyck.

Iceboxes in cities were refilled with a fresh cake by the iceman who passed every day. The icebox at our house was replenished every two or three days when Dad picked up a fresh block of ice at the ice house in town. That reminds me of the afternoon Dad and I headed for Monroe to sell some cotton.

On the way we passed a young Negro boy walking along the roadside carrying a twenty–pound block of ice, hanging in a halter made of baling twine. We stopped to give him a ride and tied the block of ice to the front bumper of the car.

It was a 100–degree August day and when we let the boy out at his home five miles on up the road, the twenty–pound block of ice had melted to ten pounds. The boy looked at the diminished block of ice and said, "Ain't nothing no good no more, look de way dat ice done melted."

On Saturday night Dad would bring home an extra big block of ice. We would make ice cream and serve it with cake to the young schoolteachers and their husbands who were always close friends of Mother.

Back in those days our leisure time did not include television. It had not been invented yet. Our cold winter nights at home, with the outside temperature below freezing, included homework for school, but that never took more than an hour. More time was spent at our hearth, whose warm fire would cook one side and leave one side cold, listening to Mother read aloud by the light of a kerosene lamp. She was good at reading aloud. Her voice was resonant and clear. I think people always said Mother didn't talk like a Southerner because her diction was so polished. She made *Pilgrims Progress* sound as good as *Tom Sawyer*.

After we grew sleepy and it was time for bed, Mother would herd us upstairs. We would race through the frigid bedroom and jump squealing into sheets colder than anything this side of Siberia. Mother would tuck us in with a kiss and a warm and loving "goodnight." After five or ten minutes, I think the body–warmth developed between the sheets and under a blanket or two was more comfortable than under an electric blanket, provided one didn't stir outside the warmed area— or Oliver didn't pull off my covers.

John Ed, Oliver, and I slept in a huge room on the second floor. Nancy and Alice had an equally large second–floor room. Both had fireplaces, but fires were not built in them unless one of us was sick. Mother and Dad slept in a small room on the first floor. A second bedroom on the first floor and a third bedroom on the second floor were for guests.

Christmases at home were big events. Not only did we enjoy the bounty of food and fruit and candy brought home from the grocer, but our stockings always had something special we knew Mother had picked out.

During the Christmas season Mother would take the whole family to the Fort Mill grocery store in her Model T Ford and Daddy would meet us there in Boogledy, Nancy's perfect name right out of her vivid imagination, for his pickup truck, and we would fill both to overflowing with the basic family needs and every extra you can imagine: oranges, tangerines, English walnuts, coconuts, candy, and to break the sausage habit at breakfast, salted fish from a barrel.

Oliver and I were ten and eleven when Santa Claus brought us a bike to share. On the day we got it I ran over our cook's foot. Her name was Priscilla and she raised such a stink with Mother about the accident (which she properly called deliberate) that it almost spoiled the festive day.

Several years later, on the same bike, I pedaled a record twenty–two miles to Rock Hill to spend a weekend with Oliver when he was in school there.

From the time of my earliest memories, our house was brimming with people. There were my parents and my four brothers and sisters. Then radiating out from our farm was an extended family of aunts and uncles and cousins and great aunts and great uncles and third cousins seventeen times removed.

Closer to home there was another set of aunts and uncles. These were the older Negro farm workers and household help who enriched our daily lives. Most of them lived in tenant houses on our property or on neighboring farms. I liked them better than I did some of my blood kinfolks.

There were six tenant houses on our home place and two on the second farm across the creek where my grandfather had lived and where my father was raised. All of these houses were owned by my dad, and they were occupied rent free by the tenant farmers as long as they were "attached" to the farm. A typical tenant house had three rooms and was built exactly like the railroad foreman's house described earlier.

The tenant farmers either worked by the hour on the farm or they were sharecroppers. Sharecroppers contributed their labor and in return they were supplied with the land, seeds, fertilizer and mules. When the crop was gathered and sold, they shared the proceeds with the landowner, usually fifty/fifty, or halvers as it was called.

The first tenant house Dad built on the property, only 100 yards behind the main house, was for Uncle Stump and Aunt Liza, who had been household servants for Dad's parents since he was a boy. Uncle Stump's father had been a slave and Stump was taken in by my grandfather after he lost a leg from a neglected infection. He became an integral part of the household; he was a handyman, a butler, he kept the home fires burning, and he chauffeured the buggy to pick up guests at the railroad station, both at Van Wyck on the Seaboard Line just two miles away and at Springdale on a Southern Railroad spur line between York, Rock Hill and Lancaster, five miles away.

He was a comfort to Mother, as he arbitrated fusses among the children or misunderstandings between the cook and wash women. He never complained about his stump or his wooden leg, nor about the fact that his wife, Aunt Liza, was legally blind, (but not quite blind enough to miss keeping a watch over Uncle Stump when a comely young cook would come to help on holidays).

Uncle Stump would bring Aunt Liza, holding her hand, to our kitchen every morning. She would sit by the big old wood stove all day long and he would lead her back home before dark every afternoon. Her only daily duty was to churn the milk and make the butter.

I can vaguely remember, or perhaps I was told the story enough to think I remember, that one night when I was around two years old, I woke up and cried for Mother. She awoke, and as she turned to get up she saw a brilliant light from the bedroom window. Quickly she realized that it was a blazing fire at Uncle Stump's house. She shrieked "Fire!" and the whole family rushed out, only to watch helplessly as the house burned to the ground with Uncle Stump and Aunt Liza inside.

An investigation the next day revealed that both Uncle Stump and Aunt Liza had died in their bed, not from the fire, but from the blows of a blunt instrument. Uncle Stump was known to have salted away some money at his house, probably in his mattress or under a board in the bedroom. Not a single coin was found in the ashes, and a young boy he had befriended was never seen again.

Mother told me, years later, that it took a long time for her to erase the stench of burned flesh from her mind. She fought a hard personal battle with depression and was on the brink of a nervous breakdown for months afterward. It was the only time in her married life that she truly wanted to go back to York to her mother and to Dr. Miles, to her childhood home.

I was too young at the time of Uncle Stump's death to remember much about him, other than his constant presence in and out of the house, and the way he would limp along in the yard leading Aunt Liza by the hand.

I do have many memories of Huss Barber, who was also always hanging around our place. He was not a sharecropper, but he was a jack of all trades. He was the young man who laid the brick for Dad's store.

Huss was the husband of Aunt Mag, our wash woman. Huss and Aunt Mag lived in one of Dad's tenant houses a mile off the main road on the back side of the farm near Twelve Mile Creek. I never knew where he got the name Huss, but he was a hustler. He was a good brick mason and carpenter and Dad used him full time on various building projects such as a new smoke house, a garage for the cars, a shed for the tractor and other farm implements. Huss could drive a twenty–penny nail through the heart of a white oak plank without bending the nail. For some unknown reason we never called him "Uncle Huss" as we did most of the other older Negro men.

Once Huss and Aunt Mag had a big fuss. Aunt Mag left home and didn't show up for two consecutive Saturdays to wash. When she finally returned, Mother asked her what the trouble had been. Aunt Mag sheepishly said: "Miss Strauss, weren't nothin' wrong. We jus' fell out 'bout who'd pick up de bucket lid I had done dropped."

Mother usually found such occurrences amusing, as long as they did not seriously interfere with the smooth running of her household. The amount of labor involved in keeping house for five children in those days was overwhelming, and we were extremely lucky in that my dad was prosperous enough to afford a cook and a part–time seamstress in addition to Aunt Mag.

The seamstress was Aunt Ella, the wife of a tenant farmer who lived on the Yoder place, the next farm down the road. Aunt Ella was the lightest colored lady for miles around and she once told Mother that her father was a white man.

White or black, aside from Mother, she was the most intelligent woman in the community of Van Wyck. Aunt Ella was probably thirty years older than Mother but they liked each other's company so much that Aunt Ella did most of the sewing for the household while sitting in our living room and visiting with Mother.

Aside from Aunt Emma, and some of the younger ladies, and all of the Van Wyck school teachers, I believe Aunt Ella was Mother's best friend. Mother was always a great talker and could carry on a lively conversation with her for hours at a time. Aunt Ella passed away before I finished high school and I don't think her place in Mother's life was ever filled.

Uncle Warner Mobley, like Aunt Ella, was a philosopher, but I remember Uncle Warner because he represented Dad's paternalistic attitude toward his hands. This was before the days of Social Security and it makes me wonder if the good people had been left alone they could have continued their self–reliance and not have needed the helping hand of Uncle Sam in such social matters.

Dad had a retirement plan for his tenants who wanted to stay after they were worn out by the relentless labor of farming. For example, Uncle Warner Mobley was in his late 70s when Dad told him, if he wanted to, he could stay as long as he lived. Dad gave him the use of three acres of land and the help necessary to raise an annual corn crop. He also gave him a six–week–old pig every year as soon as it was weaned and could live off the slop from his kitchen table. He was given all the wood he needed for his stove and fireplace, plus any white oak trees he chose, for cutting and stripping into laths to make fishing baskets to sell.

Uncle Warner spent most of his time in his old age sitting on the banks of the Catawba River minding his line, baited with a ball of cotton mixed with corn meal, waiting for a carp or a catfish to bite. When I was in high school, I spent a lot of time sitting in his broom–swept dirt yard talking with him, but mostly listening to him.

Uncle Warner had a lot of native ability, and he had remedies for many ailments. For example, when he suffered with hemorrhoids from time to time, his fix was quick and decisive. He would fill a shallow pan with kerosene and sit in it. He said, "dem hemrods jumps back up me bottom so fast hit's like de was tied to a rubber band." The kerosene would be returned to the can for it's proper use in lanterns and lamps.

Uncle Warner not only had many remedies for sicknesses but he was also wise in mysterious ways. Once a middle–aged colored man who lived in the community died for no apparent medical reason. One day this man was working in the field and appeared to be the picture of a hardy, healthy hand, but the next day he stopped eating and died in two weeks. I had heard my parents talking about the case and the fact that the coroner insisted on an autopsy, but it had not revealed any cause for the death. I asked Uncle Warner about it and he told me that the man's wife had cast a spell on him, she had conjured him because he was playing around. He said that conjuring was an ancient and effective method that leaves no trace of a murder weapon. The ploy could be as simple as a fish–hook hanging from a tree in their yard where the man liked to sit in the shade on a hot day. Uncle Warner went on to say that the conjured person is never told that he has been conjured, but gets the message when everybody else, who seem to know, stops talking to him.

I still have a vivid picture of the last time I saw Uncle Warner. It was a warm spring day and he was sitting in his yard in a cornshuck–bottomed straight chair. His eyes were bloodshot and yellow and he could hardly move. He died a few weeks later. Dad had the doctor check on him periodically. The doctor said, "He was an old man and he appeared to have suffered from syphilis for a long time and that was the reason he never had any children."

Most of the tenant farmers that my dad employed were Negroes; I can think of very few white tenants that Dad was able to tolerate for very long. One family that sticks in my mind was the Gambles. Mr. Lon Gamble was the blacksmith and spent most of his time shoeing the mules and horses and fixing the farm machinery. His two big sons did most of the field work tending to their cotton crop.

Another was Mr. Olsen. He often asked Dad for help in trying to discipline his unruly son, David.

On the last of these occasions Dad, Mr. Olsen, David, and I were in a shed by the barn. David was mad because his dad wouldn't give him any money for a weekend trip he planned to take. The boy cursed his dad. When my dad told the boy never to do that again in his presence, the young redneck made a serious mistake by cursing Dad.

Dad said no more. He looked around and picked up a five–foot–long 2 x 4 and smashed that lad over the shoulder with such a hard blow it seemed to shake the barn. It hurt me to watch. Dad said, "Never put your foot on this property again." Then he repeatedly beat the boy as he chased him across the barnyard and through the gate.

Dad told Mr. Olsen not to ever let his son return and that he himself would not be needed next year. He could pack up after his crops were laid by next month and leave.

I was shivering in my boots. I was afraid that both Olsens would turn on us and that Mr. Olsen and his big strong boy could have bested us. But they left the farm soon afterward, and we never saw them again.

As you would expect from Mother's upbringing and her job as a schoolteacher, the best education for her children was always foremost in our household. By the time I came along in 1917, John Ed was eight years old and already in school. For several years he and Nancy attended the same school in Van Wyck where Mother had taught. She knew from firsthand experience about the shortcomings of that school, so to compensate she and Dad hired a young, live–in tutor, a Miss Martin. She lived in a guest room in the house and we all saw too much of the smart and cranky lady. She lasted only one year. She was entirely too bossy, and when she tried to expand her territory beyond the supervision of the children's education and into the kitchen, Mother dismissed her.

Another year passed, and after Oliver breezed through the first and second grades, Mother decided the school at Van Wyck was unsatisfactory for her children, so she and Dad undertook a drastic restructuring of our education. It was 1923; Daddy was prosperous enough to afford a second house, and he bought an "education" home in Rock Hill. The new plan was for Mother and the children to commute to Rock Hill early on Monday mornings and return to Van Wyck on Friday afternoons. John Ed was in the ninth grade, Nancy in the fifth, Oliver in the third, and I was just entering the first grade. Alice wasn't old enough for school. Mother enrolled all of us in a semi–private school that was run by Winthrop College as a teacher's training school, the same Winthop College where Mother had gone for two years herself.

Rock Hill was twenty–two miles from Van Wyck. It was possible to travel a much shorter distance of ten miles to Rock Hill if one was willing to brave a

Catawba River crossing on a one–car ferry, installed after the nearby river bridge was washed away in 1912.

Crossing the river by ferry was an interesting experience, although we usually didn't travel that way. Normally, we would take the longer but more dependable road and cross on the river bridge, north at Fort Mill. Occasionally, however, we would decide to take the "short–cut" and would rattle down to the ferry crossing. The ferry always seemed to be on the other side, the Rock Hill side, where the operator lived in a nearby shack. After blowing the horn and shouting with all our might, the ferryman would bring the ferry across—provided he wasn't hunting or fishing five miles away.

The ferry was actually a barge, tethered to an overhead cable that stretched from one bank to the other, forty feet above the river. There were two tethers, one at either end of the barge, both fitted with pulleys to run on the cable above. Propulsion was provided by water power: movement of the ferry was accomplished by manually adjusting the outer reach of the ferry upstream by eight or ten feet. This caused the ferry to present itself at an angle of about twenty degrees to the swift river current, which pushed it to the far shore. When the stream was docile, motion of the ferry was augmented by poling. A long pole was placed on the bottom of the river from the forward end of the ferry, and the ferryman would walk aft while pushing against the pole, and in the process he helped push the ferry forward.

Landing was accomplished by slowly releasing the forward rope just before the ferry came in contact with the opposite shore. The car aboard descended a ramp onto the shore road and motored off toward Rock Hill. It was fun just to sit in the car and watch or get out and watch and get in the way.

Our home in Rock Hill was a modest four–bedroom house conveniently located a half–block from the school. My main memories of the time we spent there have to do with leaving my classroom at mid–afternoon on Fridays and racing the half–block home where Mother and Alice were waiting for us with the car packed and the engine running, ready to roll back to Van Wyck, to Dad and the dogs, there to delight in a daylong Saturday hunt for quail far out in the fields with Oliver and John Ed and a visiting cousin or two, far from the city life.

Then every Monday morning Mother's wake–up call would come: "Five o'clock! Time to get up and head back to camp in Rock Hill." Before daylight Mother would pile us all into the 1923 Model T for the trip back to a proper education.

Our second school year at the house in Rock Hill was a nightmare, and we all began to seriously wonder if a proper education was worth the trouble. Uncle Verner (the same one who drove the Stanley Steamer and set my arm) and his wife Emma had also been worried about education. They had decided that their only son Jack (who was Oliver's age and had attended his first three grades at the local school) would never get into medical school unless he got a better education.

Mother, God bless her magnanimous soul, persuaded Dad (totally against his better judgement) to allow her to invite Aunt Emma and Jack to move into our fourth bedroom and live with us during our second school year in Rock Hill.

Aunt Emma was of Mexican origin and had enough energy to fire Vern's Stanley Steamer without waiting for the boiler to heat. She could also straighten out Vern when he displeased her with a rapid volley of Spanish which only he and she understood.

Until the time of the Rock Hill experiment, Aunt Emma had been Mother's closest friend, and I think Mother was looking forward to her companionship during the long winter in Rock Hill. But something went awry. I suppose it might be possible for two families to survive under one roof, but that wasn't to be for these two families. The quarters were too close and the year too long and there were too many people for it to work. Several years passed before Mother and Aunt Emma were best friends again.

Fortunately, the Rock Hill experiment came to an early end. At the close of the second year, Mother was invited to teach again in an expanded, four–room, and better manned, or better "womaned," school at Van Wyck. Despite my interest in a sweet, pretty little girl in the second grade, it was with great joy that we all returned to our home in the country.

A couple of years later Uncle Verner got an offer to work for the state of Pennsylvania and he and Aunt Emma moved to Philadelphia, thereby solving the problem for Jack's better education. Before they left, Jack introduced Oliver and me to smoking. Jack had a good stash of smoking material hidden on a shelf behind a post in their barn. He had not only regular tobacco, but rabbit tobacco and corn silk. He offered a choice of either a pipe or paper for rolling cigarettes. It was a first class tobacco shop.

Anyone who found regular tobacco unpleasant when it was first inhaled should try inhaling rabbit tobacco or corn silks. I tried both and I needed many more smoking experiences, with a better salesman than cousin Jack, before I learned to tolerate even regular tobacco.

It was normally quiet in the country during the week. It was especially quiet on Sunday morning. A car hardly ever passed our house before Mother and Dad had the five children assembled, dressed in our best, and ready for church. If we were a little late in getting off, we would see Uncle Jim and

Aunt Beulah, who lived a quartermile up the road, chauffeured by our house in their big black Packard. A spare wheel was mounted on each front fender, ready for two flat tires, and a rear view mirror on top of each tire, ready to confirm that nothing was ever coming from behind. This would be the late call for Dad to get his brood collected and be off to church or risk missing the first hymn, usually, "Nearer My God to Thee."

I remember one particular Sunday in mid July when the peace and quiet of the morning was broken by a terrible crash just up the road from our house. We all rushed from the breakfast table and out to the roadside, where a Model A Ford lay upside down in the middle of the road, its wheels still spinning. Just as we reached the scene, one of Dad's young hired hands climbed out from under the overturned roadster.

His name was Dan Massey, and he was three sheets to the wind. We recognized the wrecked car as one that belonged to Sico, Dan's young fast track gambling friend. Having ascertained that Dan was not mortally injured, Dad got straight to the point. "Dan, this is Sico's car. Where is Sico?" Dan said: "SSSiccco ddone got sshot in a fight bbbout two hours bbback, and I's jus tttakin a lllittle rrride in his ccccar."

On that Sunday morning we missed singing "Nearer My God to Thee" and we prayed that Sico "Had a Friend in Jesus."

Daddy went to Van Wyck and fetched the magistrate, who spent the rest of the morning interviewing members of the crowd gathering where Sico's dead body lay. I don't remember how it all was finally sorted out, but Dan was not arrested and was back plowing in the fields early on Monday morning.

There didn't appear to be any need for an arrest, nor lawyers, nor a jury or a judge, just one decisive local magistrate who knew the territory.

Later that day my brother Oliver said to Dad, "We know Dan is a good driver and I'm surprised that he wrecked the car." Dad said to us, "Dan didn't wreck the car, liquor wrecked it."

Dan Massey was my favorite Negro boy. He was the son of Uncle Kudge and Aunt Bessy, tenant farmers on Dad's place. He was older than I by seven or eight years, about the age of my oldest brother John Ed. He was a strong, handsome, broad–shouldered, hardworking farm hand with a fondness for playing hard on his days off, and I suspect he fathered several children unbeknownst to him.

I must have been about twelve years old on another Sunday morning when Aunt Bessy, Dan's mother, appeared at our door. Aunt Bessy was weeping and distraught. She was hardly coherent as she tried to explain to Daddy that Dan had been in a bad fight the night before and had wound up on the sharp side of a razor. He had come home with a deep gash in his cheek from his ear lobe to his chin.

Dan had told Kudge the name of the boy who had cut him and Kudge had shouldered his shotgun and left to square things up with the other boy. Aunt Bessy said, "Kudge will shoot that no–count nigger who done cut my boy."

Dad sized up the problem and said to me: "Son, get out the car." I was tall enough to see over the steering wheel and Mother had been letting me drive the car about the place for several months. Up to that time and for a few more years a driver's license wasn't necessary in South Carolina. Dad got in with me, told Aunt Bessy to climb in, and directed me to drive to her nearby house. There he told her to get out, go in her house, try to calm down and to stay there until we picked up Kudge and brought him back.

Dad and I continued down the road toward Van Wyck and soon caught up with Kudge, carrying a shotgun over his shoulder, walking briskly toward town, headed for real trouble. We drove up beside him and I stopped the car. Daddy said, "Get in, Kudge." Kudge said, "All I was gonna do, was to see about the boy that done cut Dan so bad." Daddy said again, "Get in the car. We will go over in the morning and get the magistrate and see about the fight."

Kudge climbed in, I turned around, and we took him home. Dad said to him, "Go in the house and stay there until I come by in the morning." Kudge got out, went into his house and stayed there until the next morning.

I have often thought about this as a classic case of Dad's uncanny authority over his hands and his ability to manage and calm down a potential crisis when the consequences could have been serious.

Such Sunday morning excitement was definitely a departure from the norm. Most Sunday mornings found us, along with a majority of families, at one of three churches. The white Methodist and Presbyterian churches were the most prominent centers in the social lives of the whites. There was only one very active Negro church nearby, a half–mile or so away, the White Oak A.M.E. Zion Church. It was the largest and best–looking church in the community. As teenagers, we often attended that church on Sunday nights to hear the lively revivals with hellfire, hymns, amens and hallelujahs that peppered and enlivened the chanted sermons and raised the noise louder than at Times Square.

On a normal Sunday, I went with my parents to the staid Presbyterian service in the handsome old cathedral–like church made from Van Wyck red bricks, its front entrance overgrown with beautiful evergreen ivy vines. Just thinking about the Van

Wyck Presbyterian Church reminds me of some "almighty" stories about the place. One quip was recorded by my cousin Dan Hollis in his book *Churches In The South.*

When the Scotch–Irish Presbyterians migrated down from Pennsylvania to the Piedmont area of the Carolinas in the early part of the 18th century they brought with them the Ten Commandments and everything else they could get their hands on.

I remember the many hours I sat in a pew at the Presbyterian church, Sunday after Sunday, year after year, when the Reverend Mr. Brown was the preacher. I remember nothing he said, but they tell me he preached a lot about the Ten Commandments, and he only occasionally addressed the subjects of hellfire and damnation. Mr. Brown divided his time between the Van Wyck church and another small country church in Catawba, across the Catawba River. He had an early service at one church and a late service at the other. Mr. Brown lived in Rock Hill, and from that point of view he was absent from both of his church communities, thereby avoiding most of the gossip, confessions, sicknesses, sins and other trials and tribulations of his parishioners.

One tribulation that made a deep impression on me as a youngster was the first case of cancer to strike Van Wyck (at least within my memory). Mr. Bill Ashe, the owner of the brickyard, was a pillar of the village and a prominent Presbyterian. When I was about four or five, Mr. Ashe developed cancer of the mouth and had to have half of his tongue and a large part of his cheek removed. After the operation, he could talk only with great difficulty, and it was hard to understand anything he said. But he continued to come to services every Sunday and to be a pillar of the church. I remember him standing and rubbing his hands in front of a red–hot wood burning stove while the choir of four walked down the aisle singing, "Just as I Am."

For several years we shared Sunday School with the Methodist church, a short walk up the road. This longstanding arrangement ended when the Methodist congregation called a fiery young minister, just out of the seminary, to their church. Since he knew that Methodists and Presbyterians could not possibly share their different doctrines, he frowned on them sharing their facilities. At his second service in Van Wyck, he held a meeting and called for a vote to separate the two Sunday Schools. When a majority of the Methodists went along with their new minister and voted his way, the Presbyterians, representing half the congregation, walked out and never came back. With one exception. One outspoken Presbyterian lady, realizing she still had a Methodist hymnal in her hand, stormed back into the church, walked all the way down the aisle, and threw the book at the minister, saying, "We don't want your damn hymn book, either."

Revivals, or Missions as they were also called, were held at our church every year about the time that crops were laid by, a time of renewal. Dad was an elder in the church and one of his duties was to "put–up," that is, to invite the visiting minister holding the revival to stay at our house. On one such occasion, the visiting minister refused to eat a bite of the elaborate supper Mother had prepared.

The minister said, "I apologize for not eating now but I would prefer to eat after the service." He went on to say, "I can't give my best sermon if I eat a heavy meal before preaching." Mother didn't go to the revival meeting that night. She put his meal away to be heated and served it to him later.

When the preacher returned and was eating his late meal in the dining room and Dad was in the kitchen alone with Mother, she asked, "Edwin, did he preach a good revival sermon tonight?" Dad said, "He might as well have ett."

Mr. Brown died a few years after I left Van Wyck, and a fiery young seminarian was auditioned for the call to be the new minister.

A few ladies of the church were passing by a few days later and saw the ambitious young parson freshening up the appearance of the building. He had ropes fastened to the top of the ivy vines and with his car doing the pulling, he was relieving the church of that particular decoration.

That prospective preacher returned to the school from whence he came as fast as his legs could carry him. The ladies persuaded the Lord not to call him to lead that particular congregation.

When I was about five years old, a new item was added to our family's Sabbath rituals: the Sunday afternoon visit to Uncle Jim and Aunt Beulah.

Uncle Jim had four brothers: Dad's father, and uncles Olin, Jule and Verner. He had grown up in Van Wyck, the son of Dr. Newton Nisbet. He, like Verner and Olin, had followed in his father's footsteps by becoming a medical doctor, but rather than carry on his father's country practice, he went to Germany for graduate studies, wrote a book about the diseases of the stomach, and settled in New York City for a long and prosperous career.

Uncle Jim's given name was James Douglas Nisbet—the same as mine. I was given the name at Uncle Jim's request. He and his wife, Aunt Beulah, had been married for many years with no children, and they wanted an heir to carry on his name. My parents agreed, and I was christened James Douglas II.

Uncle Jim's return to Van Wyck made a big impression on me and everyone else. It began when he and Aunt Beulah arrived in Van Wyck traveling in a private railroad car. The car was parked on the brickyard siding and they lived there for five days while their belongings were taken by wagon to their new home.

Before retiring, Uncle Jim had accumulated 2,000 acres of land on the Catawba River, about half a mile up the road from our place. Part of this he had inherited from his father, the rest he had purchased, including the house where he had grown up. When Uncle Jim returned, the house was occupied by his mother, Mary Jane, his bachelor brother, Julius Marcellus (whom we called Uncle Jule), and his niece, Aunt Loma. Uncle Jule managed the farm and Aunt Loma managed the house and took care of her grandmother.

After Uncle Jim and Aunt Beulah moved into the old home place, they hired new servants, they relieved Aunt Loma of running the household, and relieved Uncle Jule of running the farm. My great grandmother Mary Jane, the matriarch of the clan, must have wondered whether she might be the next to go.

Uncle Jim had not been home long when he had Uncle Jule gather all the farm hands, the household help, tenants and sharecroppers to hear about his plans for developing his plantation into the finest in the South. Uncle Jim stood in front of the assembled workers in his cutaway suit, with red face and watering eyes, his bald head shining. After finishing his oration, he decided to engage in a little conversation with his captive audience. Approaching one of the elderly field hands, he asked: "How many children do you have, Isaac?" The old Negro, with a twinkle in his eye and a wealth of human psychology in his head, answered: "Well, Dr. Jim, I reckon I has somin' like 'bout eighteen beknownst to me." A strange expression came over the face of Aunt Beulah, Uncle Jim's Yankee wife, as she strained to understand this foreign lingo spoken by the black farm hand.

We, on the other hand, were trying to understand Aunt Beulah. She was a case study. Looking back, I can see that she was trying to adjust to southern ways unfamiliar to her upbringing, but she had a strange way of going about it. One of the first things she did after arriving was put a lock on everything in sight. From then on, we never saw her without a huge bunch of keys which she kept on a chain securely fastened around her waist. My sister Nancy said, "I never knew what a lock was for before Aunt Beulah came." We never locked the outside doors of our house, much less the inside doors, and it was hard for us to believe that the cook had to ask for the pantry to be unlocked before she could bake a cake. The chauffeur had to ask for the keys before he could wash the cars.

Aunt Ella, our seamstress, who also did sewing for Aunt Beulah, reported that when she ran out of thread, Aunt Beulah would unlock a cabinet, take out a spool, rethread the needle, then lock the spool back up. I think she thought she was protecting Douglas, as she called Uncle Jim. In time she developed a kindness and generosity toward us, but she never let go of those keys.

As soon as Aunt Beulah was sure that the pantry and the library and everything else in sight was securely locked, she invited Dad and Mother and us five kids to come on Sunday afternoon for a visit. That visit on the big front porch in 1922 was the beginning of a Sunday afternoon ritual that lasted for eleven years.

It was there at a tender age that I learned that children were to be seen but not heard unless spoken to. I remember Uncle Jim, standing in his striped pants and cutaway coat and high white starched collar that tickled his jaws and pressed on his Adam's apple, speaking with gusto and tearing eyes about politics, indolent tenant farmers, farm prices, poor crops, lack of rain, cold weather, hot weather, and with an occasional inquiry to my dad as to how that poor man down the road could ever make ends meet when he got drunk every Saturday night and had no apparent means of support.

It was at this first Sunday afternoon visit that Uncle Jim asked Dad to take on the management of his farms. Uncle Jule was present, and Dad said he thought Uncle Jule was secretly smiling at the plight that Dad was walking into. Uncle Jule continued to hunt and fish as he had always done.

He taught John Ed how to be a happy outdoorsman and to adopt his quiet philosophical outlook toward life. Uncle Jule died two years after Uncle Jim returned, at the age of fifty–five.

Aunt Beulah always tried to soften the harshness of the visits. She offered Sunday afternoon refreshments, something to look forward to, always the same: half ginger ale and half grape juice, recently unlocked from the pantry, plus two pieces of chocolates from a fresh box of candy far superior to Whitmans Sampler. She also always offered to lend us a copy of one of her latest books that had arrived during the week. Every week more books came to freshen the stock of her extensive 5,000 volumes. She never seemed to find places on the library shelves for the last eight or ten copies of the Book of the Month Club selections, so they were stacked on the floor or placed on the large library table. Aunt Beulah had given me a subscription to the National Geographic for as long as I remember and I didn't seem to find time to read even that, much less new books, when it was time to play. But my sisters, Alice and Nancy, were ardent readers and they frequently found new selections to borrow and take home.

Uncle Jim was a complex character. He was without any doubt a very successful professional doctor. When he returned to Van Wyck with an ailing heart, he tried to retire, to be a gentleman farmer and to join a community which he never really knew nor understood. After Uncle Jim returned to his home place and took charge of the land, he started a building program that never ended. He added a large north wing to the homestead, and later a new south wing. In the mid–1920s, he installed a modern automatic Delco 32–volt lighting system and his home was the only one in all the countryside with electric lights. He bought an automatic churn and cream separator. He built three new solid white–oak barns around the farms.

He still was restless, and turned his mind to a charitable community project. He completely rebuilt Dr. Newton Nisbet's old home place, where he was born, and gave it, with twenty–five acres of land, to the community of Van Wyck as a clubhouse. Dad called the place "Uncle Jim's Folly." The clubhouse was fitted with a new kitchen, two grass tennis courts, and a complete complement of baseball gear for two teams.

It was in that clubhouse, along with many others old and young, that I learned to square–dance to the hot tunes of Mr. Will Crenshaw's fiddle. "Lady around the gent and the gent goes slow, Gent around the lady and the lady don't go." Or something like that.

For a year or two, there was much enthusiasm for the place, enhanced by ball games, picnics and dancing to Mr. Will's fiddle. But in the 1930s as the Depression deepened, a general gloom settled over the community. Times were too hard for play. After Uncle Jim passed away in 1933, the Van Wyck Community Club experienced a long slow death.

My dad stuck with Uncle Jim and his idiosyncracies through many changes in plans, from fencing the entire farm for cattle, to building a hog barn on each place for hog farming, from planting only cotton, to only corn to only wheat. All the time Dad was trying to keep up with the management of his own two farms. It was a full plate.

After a few years of this unsuitable arrangement of being a hired manager, Dad tried renting Uncle Jim's land and then was almost able to manage it to suit himself, although Uncle Jim continued to look over his shoulder. The crowning blow came in 1929 and 1930 when the bottomland corn crop was lost two years in a row and Uncle Jim would make no concessions for the rent. Dad never completely recovered from that financial debacle, and with educational expenses for his brood of five staring him in the face, I suspect he wondered about the wisdom of choosing farming as a career.

Farming is a highly seasonal activity. In the fresh spring of the year the soil is turned and planted. In the hottest part of the summer the crops are chopped and plowed and plowed again and finally laid by. In the brisk fall of the year the crops are gathered in.

On our farm, the main crops were grain, hay, and cotton. The grain was gathered and some of it was sold, but most of it was stored. The hay was mowed and raked then hauled to the barn and stacked in the loft where it cured to what the cows and the mules must have considered a tasty brown. Most of the grain and hay was stored for the winter feeding of dozens of hungry mouths: the cows, the horses, the mules, the sheep, the goats, the hogs, and the turkeys. Oh, and the chickens, Rhode Island Reds, White Leghorns and Bantam roosters, with a couple of Guinea hens scattered among the flock to add variety by cackling to a different tune.

When the cotton matured in the early fall, it was picked, ginned and baled. The heavy white bales were frequently sold to the cotton gin owner or to brokers who collected it and resold it by the boxcar load to the textile mills in New England. Sometimes, if Dad thought the price would be higher six months after harvesting, he would not sell his cotton immediately after it was ginned, but would hold it for the possibility of a better price.

On one occasion that I remember, he had withheld about fifty bales and we took samples to my mother's cousin Sid Walker for an offer. Sid was a cotton buyer in Monroe. From the daily quote in the paper, Dad knew the going price for cotton, but he didn't know what his cotton would bring until he took samples to be "pulled" to measure the staple. A skilled cotton buyer could "pull" cotton between the thumb and forefinger of each hand and tell the staple, the length of the cotton fibers, within a fraction of an inch without a ruler. Dad's cotton pulled well that day, and he sold his fifty bales to Sid Walker for a much better price than he would have received six months before.

I think Dad enjoyed trading even more than he enjoyed farming. He particularly liked to trade horses and mules and cows. There were not many people around who could get the best of him in a trade. Once he went in halvers with Henry Collins, the livery stable operator in Waxhaw, and they bought and divided a boxcar load of untrained mules from Tennessee. Daddy used his farm help, during the leisurely fall months, to break and train his mules. Then the trading began. A mule for a cow or for a sow with a new litter of pigs, or for a bunch of billy goats that Mother thought were the nastiest and smelliest animals to come off Noah's ark.

When cold winds blew in from the north and the first frost whitened the pastures, we always knew it was November, and hog–killing time on the farm. Killing hogs was a ritual that began at the crack of dawn, and I can still picture the scene as clearly as if I were there.

There is frost covering the pastures, and even though the sun has yet to rise above the trees, the barnyard is a bustle. Kindling and logs are laid in a shallow pit and lighted to start a fire. A huge kettle of water is placed on stones above the fire and the water is brought to a boil, to sit and wait for the first hog.

Dan Massey lures the first hog from the barn with a bucket of slop. He sets the bucket on the ground near the fire, straddles the hog and raises his axe. When the hog stops slurping the slop and raises its head for a breath of air, Dan aims behind its snout and between its ears and hits it squarely on the head with the flat side of the axe. The hog's legs wither and it falls to the ground. Dan unsheathes a razor–sharp knife from a holster tied to the hammer slot on his overalls and slits its throat.

The dogs that are always lazing about dash to the scene and lap up the blood as it pulsates from the quivering neck of the hog in harmony with the dying beat of its heart.

With Uncle Kudge and Uncle Levy helping, the dead hog is lifted, lowered into the kettle of boiling water, and scalded from its snout to its curly tail. Its hair that had shone so black and bright in the early morning sun loses its sheen as it is scraped away from the hide, down to the last whisker, until the clean white hide of the hog glows.

A stick is placed between the hamstrings of the hog's hind legs and fitted with a rope and tackle hanging from the limb of a nearby tree. The hog is raised, head down, to just above the ground. Then its belly is slit open and the liver, the kidneys and the heart are retrieved to be cooked later into a liverwurst stew.

The other entrails are cut free and fall into a wheelbarrow below the hanging snout of the hog. Sometimes the intestines are taken away by the hands to be cleaned for chitlin treats. Otherwise, the wheelbarrow is rolled a couple of a hundred yards into the nearby field and dumped.

Next day, the early morning sun taints the decaying mess, and soon the pungent stink rises to the keen nostrils of the buzzards that always soar above, always alert to the scent of a juicy meal. They spiral down, directed by the rising scent, like the pilot of a plane on an instrument landing system, and join the feast on the morning after hog–killing day.

After the hog is rendered, the work is only just beginning. The head is cut off at the neck and boiled for about four hours and then the bones and teeth and cartilage are lifted free of the meat. This mixture is stirred with sage and salt and other herbs to make hog jowl. (People in Philadelphia call it scrapple.)

The remaining carcass is cut in half and taken to the kitchen for more work. After the fat is cut away, the lean meat is cut from the ribs and ground into sausage. The sausage is salted and seasoned with a generous portion of sage, pressed into patties, cooked and preserved in Mason jars with hot lard.

Extra lard is boiled with lye and ashes from the fire and cast into a flat dish. When it has cooled and hardened, the cake is cut into squares of soap.

All the hogs from the day's slaughter are cut into hams and shoulders, rubbed with a brine solution, and hung for two nights in the smokehouse. Then they are wiped clean, coated with a slurry of brown sugar and molasses, and hung again in the smokehouse.

The floor of the smokehouse is covered with smoldering coals which are not allowed to flame and are often replenished with fresh coals from the hickory fire maintained outside. The pungent odor of white hickory smoke, darkened a shade or two by the vapors given off from the sugared molasses solution, seeps from the cracks around the ceiling of the smokehouse with a look and a smell that a little boy can never forget. In five or six days, the hams and shoulders are cured and good for many a hearty meal on cold winter nights.

The fresh sausage is always sampled at breakfast the next morning. To round out the meal there are eggs from the hen house, grits from freshly ground corn, biscuits from freshly milled wheat, and sweets to choose from; jam from the orchard fruits, molasses from the sugar cane patch, or honey from John Ed's bee hives.

Why not be a farmer? Farmers eat high on the hog!

Another special event took place on our farm once a week. For several years Dad had known a grocery and meat market merchant in nearby Fort Mill and had sold him a cow from time to time. The merchant's butcher would come to our farm and pick up the live cow in a Model T truck and return home to butcher it.

Daddy suggested a simpler plan. He would supply one or two cows a week to be butchered on Friday afternoon at our farm under the direction of the butcher and with the help of two or three hands, Oliver and John Ed and me, the jacks of all trades.

The butchered cow would be weighed and priced and the value credited to Dad's account. Dad in turn agreed to buy most of the groceries for our family from the merchant and that bill would be debited. The debits and credits were to be balanced once a month and any differences would be settled with cash passed one way or the other. The merchant and Dad shook hands on this barter deal and it worked well for many years.

Daddy fed the family with the food chain beginning with corn and hay grown on the farm and fed to cattle that were butchered and traded to the grocer for an overabundance of groceries. And as fringe benefit, we three boys got to be pretty good at butchering cows.

There were a few differences between rendering cows and butchering hogs. The cow was usually killed with a .22 rifle, but I like the axe better because the .22 bullet often got lodged in the brain, and it isn't appetizing to find a bullet mixed with your brains, scrambled eggs and grits at breakfast.

One of my jobs was to saw open the cow's head between the eyes and the horns to recover the brains. Inspection at that time usually revealed the bullet, if the cow had been shot. The tongue was also removed and kept. Sometimes Daddy would carve out a big chunk of T-bone steaks for our breakfast the next morning. I never knew until long after I left home that the meat of a cow was supposed to be "aged" a week or ten days before being eaten.

Another big difference between preparing a cow and a hog was that the cow was skinned rather than scraped and the hide was sold to be tanned for leather. Sometimes, brother John Ed, who was truly a jack of all trades, would tan the hides himself. He got the tannic acid for the job by crushing black walnut hulls gathered from a tree in our front yard. After soaking the hides for ten days and making a general mess, he would produce leather good enough to sell.

The brains, the heart and the liver of the cow were eaten as special dishes rather than mixed and stewed into someone's messy paté. The cow's hoofs were sold to the glue factory, whereas:
the pig's feet were pickled
and preserved in a Mason jar
for food far better than caviar.

In addition to cows and hogs, Dad also raised sheep for a while. The biggest customers for his sheep were members of the Jewish community in Charlotte. They usually bought lambs on the hoof, but sometimes they came with their rabbi to butcher the animals on the farm.

To make the meat of the lambs kosher, the rabbi would bless it with strange signs drawn in the air. Then he would stand around in his black hat and stroke his beard and watch without mussing his hands with blood while the sheep was freshly sheared, then hung by its heels for the ritual slitting of its throat.

My two brothers and I became very good butchers. We would not have hesitated to tackle a cow; a small calf anyway.

As a result of our butchering experience, Dad gave my brother Oliver a chance to try his hand at a small business enterprise when he was in his teens. The deal was a straightforward business proposition and a perfect example of Dad's shrewd way of teaching his boys about business with real life experiences.

The deal with Oliver was structured like this: Oliver would pick out a fat young steer from the herd about noon on Friday, then he and Dad would agree on the price, on–the–hoof. The terms allowed two days of credit, with payment due in full on Sunday morning.

Oliver would hire Dan Massey and corral me to help him butcher the cow on Friday afternoon. The cow would age overnight, hanging from the tree where it was butchered.

Before daylight on Saturday morning, Oliver would borrow two mules and a wagon from the barn. He would load the beef, cover it with old sheets, mount a chopping block on the back of the wagon, and store knives, a saw, and an axe in the wagon for further processing the meat. A stack of old newspapers was added for wrapping the meat when it was sold.

Off he and Dan would go up the road, followed by a swarm of flies, toward the settlements of Oceola, Bellair, Pleasant Valley and throughout the township of Indian Land. They would sell the meat house to house, country store to country store, baseball lot to baseball lot, from Negro tenant farmer to white trash to anybody who might be passing along the road.

Oliver and Dan did this for two summers, and I never remember them returning home with any leftover meat. When they arrived back in the yard, always well after dark, Oliver would pay off Dan, fifty cents or seventy–five cents if the profits were extra fat that day. It was never too late on Saturday night for Dan to head back to Van Wyck to dance and play and fight.

Then at breakfast on Sunday morning Oliver would pay off his debt to Dad for the steer and pocket a profit of $10 to $15. For Oliver, this experience, beef on wheels, was better than an M.B.A. from Harvard. It was on the job training; buying, selling, managing, and finance. For the rest of his life, Oliver always seemed to know the value of a dollar.

When Oliver was running his rolling butcher shop, the fact that he bought steers from Dad, rather than bulls, heifers or cows, needs more explanation.

About half of the cows born are bulls, but that many bulls are not needed to mingle with the cows and satisfactorily propagate the herd. The fact is, a very few bulls can take care of a large number of heifers.

So every spring when our crop of newborn calves was six or eight weeks old, the pick of the bulls, sometimes two, were selected for breeding. All the other bull calves were corralled for a Saturday morning castration ceremony, after which the initiates are officially declared steers!

Steers are tamer and grow bigger and fatter and are better beef cattle than a philandering bull. It's another manmade way to provide the equivalent of steroid shots to increase the appetite and speed up the metabolism and add weight.

The way that we transformed bulls into steers gets a little clinical. The young bulls were penned in the barnyard and brought out one by one. Dan would straddle the bull at the neck. While he held it, immobilized, either Oliver or I would clean and sterilize its sack with a quick pass of a cloth wet with alcohol. Then Daddy moved in with a razor–sharp linoleum knife and as quickly as you can say, "Oh my aching balls," he would slit the bag and cut loose the testicles. Kudge, standing nearby, would lift a paint brush from a bucket of creosote and swab the incision black with a protective coat of tar. Dan would let go and the new steer, its tail held high in the air, would prance off into the field and bleat three times, in high C.

On the farm sex education was *au naturel*. When I was a boy, we always had flocks of chickens running loose in the yard, only to be penned just before dark so they could roost in the chicken house, protected from the fox, who loved a midnight chicken supper.

I suppose I was only three or four years old when Mother and I were out in the yard feeding the chickens. A hen dashed from the flock. In a split second the rooster hopped on her back and firmly clasped his legs around her body. He kept his balance by seizing the top of the hen's head with his bill. They squatted and squirmed and wiggled around a few times as if seeking a more comfortable position.

Then the rooster hopped off and crowed. The hen slowly stood up and walked calmly away, clucking to herself, as if satisfied she had carried the day.

I said, "Mother, I have seen the rooster and the chickens play like that before. What is that all about?"

Mother, with absolute dignity, self–confidence and authority, said: "It is the way nature has arranged to fertilize the hen's eggs. Otherwise the eggs would not hatch into little chicks."

This was a straight, simple, and very satisfying answer for a little boy, a sex education in two sentences. Nothing more needed to be said. I had enough imagination to broaden that observation of reproductive behavior to many other barnyard scenes I had observed—the natural copulation of the boar and the sow and the bull and the cow, and horses, goats, sheep, cats, dogs, rabbits and squirrels, too.

Later on when I was in school, I got a less gentle lesson. I didn't know then what the legal word "entrapment" meant, but in recent years, after learning the definition of the word, I now realize that when I was in the seventh grade I was subjected to a case of entrapment.

After a pick–up baseball game had ended on the school playground and six or eight of the older players were gathered on the benches by the field, a senior named Luther Gamble took charge.

He said to me, "Jim, I bet you ain't old nough to ever done played with yoself." (English wasn't the best subject in our country schools at that time.) I blushed and didn't answer him but I had a funny feeling that more was to come. Luther, having carefully prearranged this drama, looked at the other older boys, laughed, and continued, "I hear tell that if anybody ever done jacked off, he'll have a hair right in the middle of the palm of his hand." I bit, hook, line and sinker, opened my hand and looked at my palm. The older boys fell from the benches with laughter.

In addition to the larger farm crops of cotton, corn, wheat, oats and barley, secondary crops played an important part in our farm livelihood and in our special celebrations. I am not thinking of the large variety of household foodstuffs that came from the vegetable garden nor the fruits from the orchard, but of two very special crops that rounded out our table: sugar cane and watermelon.

An acre or two in the sandiest soil on the farm was always set aside for the watermelon and cantaloupe patches. When the melons started to ripen, it was a popular patch not only for our family and the tenants, but also for poachers and animals and birds. No matter how many scarecrows we hung, the birds always got their share. They all seemed to know there is no better eating on the farm than the taste of a sweet watermelon cut early in the morning when the cool dew still wets the vine.

Another three acres was always designated for the sugar cane patch whence came homemade molasses. Early in the fall of the year, soon after the first frost, the cane was cut and hauled to a field near the barn and stacked in a pile, to wait until the local molasses cooker could schedule his equipment for molasses–making at our place.

The equipment for sugar cane processing was basic and quite simple. It consisted of a machine with two adjustable vertical drums that rotated in opposite directions. Sugar cane stalks were squeezed flat and dry between the tight drums and the sweet sap drained into a holding keg below. This rotating press was powered by a mule that walked round and round, all day long, on the end of a twenty–five–foot boom that was geared to drive the drums.

The cooking equipment consisted of a huge flat pan about ten feet long, three feet wide, and four inches deep. The pan was fitted with a maze of separate passages, each about six inches wide and open on alternate ends. Water was evaporated from the liquid, which thickened as it was dragged with flat paddles from passage to passage for the entire length of the pan. Sugar cane juice was periodically poured into the entrance end of the pan to maintain a constant liquid level.

A fire box below the pan provided heat to evaporate the water and as the dross was constantly ladled away, the distilled cane juice became strong, thick molasses. The hot and sticky molasses was tapped and bottled in Mason jars, ready to sweeten a biscuit for a hungry boy.

I was always fascinated with the special parties on the farm: I think I will be a farmer after all.

On the other hand, there were certain annual occurrences that I did not look forward to. Without one doubt, the dirtiest and most uncomfortable farm chore was threshing grain. Whether it was wheat, oats, barley, or millet, the job was damn dirty.

Here was the scene. The Farmall tractor was stationed twenty feet from the thresher. A six-inch wide belt stretched from the drive pulley on the tractor to the driven pulley on the thresher. Hands standing on a wagon threw freshly-cut shocks of grain to hands feeding the thresher.

At the bottom back side of the thresher, grain poured from an auger into a bucket. The bucket was emptied into sacks which were sewed shut with two "ears" hanging out the top for handling. The straw, now stripped of the grain, was blown out the back end of the machine.

The entire operation was shrouded in a sticky, heavy dust called chaff. The favorite place for the chaff to land and settle was on the sweaty bare skin of the workers, beneath the inner layers of our clothing. That is the uncomfortable fact that made threshing grain the sweatiest and itchiest and most uncomfortable of all jobs on the farm.

Invention–minded "McCormicks" of the present day have eliminated the old stationary threshing machine and replaced it with a traveling harvester driven by one man riding in an air–conditioned cab, listening to country music, or opera if he prefers, on an FM radio. The self–propelled harvester proceeds down the rows faster than a man can walk. It cuts and threshes the stalks and sends the grain into a truck traveling alongside. The straw is baled and dumped along the way. The wind drives the chaff across the field where there are no bodies for it to itch.

Apart from minor irritants like wheat chaff, I hardly remember a care in the world during my childhood and teen years on the farm. I must have worried about something, but looking back now I don't know what it could have been.

On second thought, there was one summer when I had plenty to worry about. It was during the summer of 1931 when Dad decided to give me my first real experience with the business of farming. I think Dad already knew that while I was attracted to all the pleasures of living on the farm, except for doing the minor chores of feeding the stock and milking the cows and selling a sheep or a pig from time to time, for cash of course, I never had been drawn to working or pulling my own weight.

I explained how Dad gave Oliver his advanced education by setting him up in a weekend butcher business. John Ed was already managing his own peach orchard. Dad thought I was ready at a rather early age, too. I was only 14 years old. It was in the spring of the year and planting time had arrived.

Dad said, "Jim, you always wanted to do a little sharecropping on your own, so I am going to give you five acres of ground up the road next to John Ed's peach orchard. You can plant it in cotton. I'll furnish the ground, the seeds, the fertilizer, the boll weevil poison, lend you one mule as needed, and you can hire Dan to help you on Saturdays. We will share equally in the cotton crop you raise."

That was it, a simple deal with Dad. On my own, all summer, I figured I'd raise a bale an acre. Five 500-pound bales of cotton = 2,500 pounds; at ten cents a pound, that would come to $250. If I could get Dan for fifty cents a day, that would be my only expense, not counting my own labor. Then I would owe Dad $125 and keep the rest.

Raising cotton involved three months of hard work. First I had to turn over the field with a turnplow, which took a foot–deep bite of soil and returned it bottom side up. Then I smoothed the field with a mule–drawn drag harrow. We had to make several passes to pulverize the clods. Next Dan and I laid out rows thirty inches apart with a small mule–drawn plow that opened a shallow furrow.

Once the furrows were made, it was time to fertilize. Dad loaned me his fertilizer applicator, which was basically a big funnel. I would fill a twenty–pound bag of fertilizer and strap it over my shoulder, dip in with my right hand and pour the fertilizer into the funnel with my left hand. The bag held just enough fertilizer to make one round trip across the field, down one row and back up the next one. The trick was to dispense the fertilizer at the right rate so that the round trip was accomplished with all the fertilizer deposited as the trip ended, but not before and with none left over. I almost always gave out early or had some left over.

When that dusty job was over, Dan and I got the mule back out, hooked up a contraption called the cotton planter, and planted the seed. That part was fun.

Then I prayed for rain. Eighty percent of the seeds will sprout into what is called "a good stand" of cotton. Dad could grade a stand from the side of the road early in the morning of the first day that the seedlings broke ground. A week after I planted my field Dad pronounced my crop to be only a "fair stand" and doubted that I would make five bales.

I didn't have very much time to worry about whether he was right, because pretty soon it was time to chop the cotton. Chopping cotton consisted of repeatedly pulling a six–inch wide hoe across the row, leaving new little cotton sprouts standing six inches apart, down each row and back and on across the field.

Plowing resumed with a small side–plow, two passes between each row. This removed weeds that were enjoying the fertilizer and competing with the cotton. This plowing had to be done two or three times until the cotton bloomed. Then the crop was said to be "laid by", meaning that the ground work was complete and the effort shifted to poisoning boll weevils.

All the chores in raising a cotton crop are bad, but poisoning was the messiest and stickiest job of all. A drum of poison was placed at the end of each five or six dozen rows. The poison was a mixture of arsenic dissolved in molasses. We dispensed it across the top of each cotton stalk with a mop made of rags on the end of a pole, frequently dipped into a gallon pail of poison we carried in the other hand. The practice was analogous to that of a Catholic priest blessing his congregation with holy water.

Again, the trick of metering the poison takes practice: the pail is supposed to run dry at the end of a round trip down one row and back up another. And on and on across the field.

The carp and catfish swimming in the branches, in Twelve Mile Creek, and in the Catawba River probably didn't appreciate the taste of arsenic in their water. But there was no E.P.A. in those days to measure such things in parts per million, or is it parts per billion?

Finally the cotton was picked and that is not a task for an aching back.

The summer was long. The sun was too hot. It didn't rain enough. The boll weevils were hungry. I couldn't always get Dan to work for me on Saturdays. I finally picked one bale of cotton from amongst four wagon loads of weeds. I made up my mind: I was not going to be a farmer.

We didn't work on the farm every waking moment in the summer. We spent many hours swimming in the pond Daddy built. That swimming pond was a big undertaking. It covered at least two acres and was built by constructing a dirt dam on a branch several hundred yards behind our house. That was before the days of bulldozers and heavy earthmoving equipment, so the dam was built with six hands driving six mules pulling six drag–pans that held about half a yard of dirt. A few thousand pan loads eventually added up to a ten–foot high dirt dam which backed up enough water for a swimming pool.

Mother loved to swim. She swam the side stroke and could race with the best of us. She would hop in and swim for an hour without stopping. Except for Dad, who didn't swim very much, the rest of us would swim almost every day, and on some days Oliver and I would swim in the morning and again in the afternoon. Of course, we always had to be on the alert for an occasional cottonmouth water moccasin, but we didn't mind having turtles swimming along with us. Late during the first summer we had the pond, Mother had to cancel her daily swim because she broke her arm skating on the front porch. She was certainly a lively lady.

Nancy, my older sister, and Alice, my younger sister, did their share of swimming and they also did a lot of horseback riding with Mother. I am not sure my sisters had their own horses, but there always seemed to be horses resting in the barn while the mules were out pulling plows. Mother gave up her side saddle for the English saddle and my sisters rode on western saddles.

Nancy and Alice were enthusiastic about some of our farming activities, like molasses–making, but they didn't have farm chores. I don't think they even helped me milk the cows. They wrote poetry and short stories and loved to read. Alice was a bookworm who would retreat to her room to read when company would come. Mother had to retrieve her from her room to come down and speak to Aunt Emma, or Aunt Loma, or Aunt Emma Lee, or Aunt Evelyn, or Aunt Olive, or Aunt Mary, when they came to call.

Nancy lived a sad life for many years. When she was a junior at Winthrop College, she developed tuberculosis. When she was at Winthrop, she edited the college newspaper. Dad built a huge screened porch on the inside corner of our T–shaped house. There Nancy stayed in bed for long periods of time, until the case was arrested and she could resume her education. She was always fun to be around and we enjoyed her company even though, as one would expect, she was sad and restless at times.

From time to time in summer Mother would shout to all of us: "Hurry, hurry, hurry up! Off the side porch in the east yard, a swarm of bees is passing. Get pots and pans and spoons from the kitchen and let's make a resounding noise."

We would all gather various noise makers and run outside in search of the bees. Sometimes the swarm would be ten feet wide, moving across the yard like a dark wide cloud, making a noise like a small jet as it moved forward at the pace of a slow walk. For some reason the clamor and din of tin pans hit repeatedly with heavy kitchen implements made an eerie sound that enticed the queen bee to light. When the queen lit, the swarm of drones and honeybees would settle protectively around her, making a large ball–of–bees that sometimes grew to be eighteen inches or so in diameter.

Settling on the limb of a tree, the ball–of–bees would grow relatively docile and quiet. Then John Ed would step in, suited in his bee outfit with gloves and a mask that covered his entire head. Pumping his smoking bellows, he would further quiet the bees.

He would then reach one arm into the midst of the swarm, rake out a handful of bees, and transfer them into one of his hives, where they would settle down, buzzing less and less as they got used to their new home. The next spring, before the crops were planted, this new hive would be full of fresh honey.

Every year in late April or early in May, Mother would gather two or three of us together in the yard and say, "Time to go find the lady's slippers and dig up some ferns." We would get a shovel and a couple of buckets and be off across the hill and on a mile or two into the woods to a particular place by a wet–weather branch. Mother could always tell when we arrived by the branch whether we were above or below the special and only spot where the lady's slippers grew. She would lead us a few yards upstream or a few yards downstream and there the lady's slippers would be, hiding under a few ferns in the moist, moss–covered soil. There were never more than three or four blooming and we would never pick more than one of the beautiful yellow blossoms to take home and enjoy; and to prove to Edwin, as Mother called him, that we had found the lady's slippers again that year.

Dad didn't have as much leisure time as we did, of course, what with managing three farms. He didn't normally hunt and fish, but in the fall of the year he would join the boys and other grown men in the nightlong fox hunt. Mr. Fred Starns was an ardent local fox hunter who always kept a dozen fox hounds and would lead the hunt on our place once or twice a year. It would start with the hunters and the dogs gathered deep in the woods, near the river. The dogs would be untied and released with one command, "Go find the fox."

The hunters would sit with their lanterns and tell stories, and smoke, and drink a little and wait, or sleep. By and by we would hear the distant barking of the dogs, several miles away tracking a fox. We would head toward the sound, following farm roads and old sawmill trails. The barking would change from tracking to baying and we would know the fox had been treed.

Eventually, after stumbling through the woods with only the light of a lantern and flashlight, we would arrive at the scene and see, reflected from a flashlight, the beady eyes of the fox peering down from high in a tree. The fox would be shot with a rifle so the damage to the fur would be less than a shotgun would cause. The dogs would be commanded again: "Go find the fox," and the hunt would be repeated. This would go on for fox after fox until the wee hours of the morning, or sometimes until daylight. I would have good long naps while waiting for the next fox.

Another diversion we always looked forward to was a trip to town with Dad. When we were young, the population of the village was 200 to 300 souls, depending on how far out in the country one counted. Van Wyck still had the same crook in the dirt road across the tracks from the brickyard. There were now five stores, still huddled together against the depot. Mr. Sam Thompson's was the busiest. Mr. Sam was the most friendly and trusted merchant. His store had the only gas pump in town. It was a gas pump in the truest sense of the word, because gas had to be pumped by hand to fill the glass tank on top of the pump. The glass tank was calibrated with a mark for each gallon and quarter–gallon and eighth–gallon.

When one of Mr. Thompson's four sons serviced a car, he would rarely sell more than two or three gallons, but when he reached the gallons purchased, he would purposely exceed the proper marker by a sixteenth of a gallon or so. The young Thompson clerk would say nothing, but the customers could see they were always getting a bonus over the full measure they had bought.

One of Mr. Sam's sons, Sheron, after clerking for his dad for several years, bought my dad's old store building and went into business for himself. Whenever we were in town on Saturday in the summertime, I would head for Sheron's store and help him turn two five–gallon freezers of ice cream that he sold for five cents a cone. One freezer was vanilla and of course the other was peach.

One Monday morning, after Sheron had been in business for a while, two strangers appeared in Van Wyck and leisurely visited all five stores while buying only one pack of Camels. On Tuesday the same two strangers returned and wandered about for all the clerks to see, then bought a pack of Chesterfields in a different store.

On Tuesday afternoon, Mr. Sam Thompson called together his four sons and the other store owners to talk about the two strangers. The merchants unanimously agreed that the strangers were thieves and planned to rob one or more of the stores. They had no way of knowing the date nor the time they would strike. Mr Sam spoke for the group:

"I think the two strangers came on Monday to survey the layouts of each of the four stores and they came back today to decide which store to rob. Each store would be equally easy to rob, in that each has a front and a side door, but robbing the store with the Post Office would be a federal offense so they might make Sheron's store their last choice. However, if I were a robber I would choose the store the owners might least expect, the store with the Post Office. Since we don't know when they will strike, we must set up a watch beginning tonight."

That night before midnight, the sheriff with half the merchants watched from a darkened room at Erskin Thompson's house near the east end of town, while the magistrate with the other half of the merchants watched from Mr. Ash's house near the west end.

At 2 a.m. on the very first night of surveillance, the two robbers appeared and broke into Sheron Thompson's store. They had not been inside more than a couple of minutes when two cars pulled up outside: one car within ten feet of the front door, and the second car within ten feet of the side door. At a signal, two sets of headlights were turned on at high–beam, and six men piled out of each car and took safe positions behind the cars with guns drawn.

Then the Sheriff shouted from the front door: "You are covered, front and back. Come out with your hands held high over your heads." The magistrate shouted the same warning from the sidedoor.

Out walked the two amateur robbers, who were handcuffed, arrested and taken to jail.

While I was growing up, things were changing in Van Wyck. The town depot, which had held such a position of importance, still stood next to the stores, but now the trains did not often tarry to park empty freight cars on the siding to be loaded with cotton and bricks, because heavy over–the–road trucks now came to town to bring the freight in and to take it away. Only every now and then would a train be flagged down for a rare passenger to get aboard, or stopped by the conductor to let a passenger off. As more people got cars, passenger stops become less frequent.

The mail still came and went by train twice every day, but the train didn't even stop for that old tradition. Some ingenious engineer had devised a method to pick up and deliver mail without stopping. The mail bag going out was fastened to a stand by the tracks and the train conductor would snare the mail bag with a hook secured to the door of the mail car as the train went by at full speed. The incoming mail bag was merely thrown from the moving train to the road side, carrying nothing fragile I hope. Both simple practical methods worked just fine.

As in all small towns, the Post Office was a central gathering spot. For most of my childhood the Post Office was located in Mr. Courtney's store, the smallest in Van Wyck, and the Postmaster was Mr. James A. Hyatt, a highly respected and well–liked citizen.

For eleven years, all was well in the Post Office, until one day the Postal Examiner came by unannounced. Mr. Hyatt, it seems, had become lax in his habit of comingling his change with the funds that belonged to Uncle Sam. He would correct any discrepancy from time to time. But a surprise audit by the unexpected inspector found a deficiency of $78.27, and Mr. Hyatt was forthwith arrested, not allowed to payup, and carted off to jail. The post office rules required a balanced account at all times.

A short time later Mr. Hyatt was tried and convicted and sent to federal prison in Atlanta. Of course Mr. Hyatt and his family were close friends with everyone in town, and everybody was served a terrible blow that took years to overcome. Mr. Hyatt, whose pride was destroyed and whose spirit was crushed beyond his endurance, committed suicide in his prison cell.

M r. Bates was the local mail carrier. He was better educated than most of the men in Van Wyck, but he suffered long spells of sickness and was often unable to deliver the mail. His teenage daughter Lucia, although not officially his assistant, often delivered it for him. Small towns have ways of getting jobs done without necessarily being official.

I was particularly fond of Lucia, even though she was older than I. When she drove her father's mail route I liked to be out at our box just to see her, and hoped she liked to see me. When I got a little older, Lucia frequently took me for a ride in her dad's Ford coupe with another young couple behind in the rumble seat. I would have preferred the rumble seat because it was a much tighter fit back there.

When I was growing up, Mr. Bates was the second man to commit suicide in Van Wyck.

One of the things about living in a small town is that your character flaws are well known to everyone, and this was especially true in the days before television and air–conditioning kept people inside their houses so much. I don't think I am romanticizing when I say that the citizens of Van Wyck had a way of tolerating and dealing with some of the rougher edges among us, including two drunks that lived in town, Mr. Kirk Yoder and Mr. James Spray.

Mr. Spray operated a sawmill and worked hard during the week back in the woods, driving a crew of three Negroes. Mr. Spray would celebrate his day off with a bottle of whiskey and would often put in an appearance in town, staggering and weaving and talking too loud among the Saturday shoppers.

One Saturday afternoon about dark, Mother and Dad, Nancy, Alice, Oliver and I stopped in Van

Wyck to pick up some groceries. As we parked the car we couldn't help but notice Mr. Spray, three sheets to the wind, among the milling crowd on the sidewalk. Dad disappeared into the store, and the rest of us sat in the car watching the Saturday afternoon scene. It wasn't long before we noticed Mr. Spray arguing with someone. The next thing we knew, he had pulled out a pistol and started shooting. We all ducked, but not before a bullet hit the side door where Mother sat and another bullet hit the arm of a Negro lady standing on the sidewalk. Erskin Thompson, who was the magistrate at the time, rushed out of his store, unarmed, and tackled Mr. Spray.

The next Saturday, and the next and the next, Mr. Spray was back on the sidewalk, but he stayed only one or two sheets to the wind for a spell.

Kirk Yoder was a different story. He and his brother Cecil were solid Methodist church–going citizens of Van Wyck. Kirk was an affable man and well–liked by all, but nobody, especially Uncle Jim, could ever figure out how he was able to live and buy liquor when he worked so little.

Kirk Yoder was a peaceful drinker and never caused any trouble. As Saturday afternoons passed into the night and before Kirk would pass out, someone would always take him to his home near the stores and his wife Miss Edna would put him to bed.

Kirk's brother Cecil was a successful merchant who had been in a partnership with Mr. Bob Massey in the Massey–Yoder Company store for many years. Their two–story store was the first to be built in Van Wyck by Mr. Massey's father. But their long–standing partnership came to a bitter end when I was about ten years old.

They had such a bad falling out that it developed into a fistfight on the sidewalk in front of their store. Mr. Cecil, being the minority partner, was thrown out and never allowed back into the store again. Mr. Cecil opened his own store, the fifth store in Van Wyck. It was located in a new wood–framed building on the east end of the group of stores and as far as one could get from Mr. Bob Massey's.

While the new building was under construction, Mr. Cecil took the first vacation he ever had and celebrated the occasion by taking his family to the Indy 500 automobile races in Indianapolis. To me at that time, Indianapolis might as well have been in India, it was such an unbelievable distance away from home.

Mr. Cecil's son Julius clerked in the new store and brought the first Magnavox radios, or were they Atwater Kent, to Van Wyck. Dad bought one of the expensive battery–powered radios and I remember on the first night we had it we were barely able to tune in WLS in Cincinnati, or was it in Chicago? We listened to static as the station faded in and out.

The radio was a real curiosity and we played it a lot for several weeks, but programming at that time was so poor it was easy to lose interest.

I suppose Van Wyck was like all small towns with respect to some of the normal accidental events of human nature. There were two illegitimate boys in town. One of the fathers was well–known because there was a shotgun wedding soon after the boy was born.

The other father was not known for sure but Dad thought he knew beyond much doubt. Both boys were near the age of my sister Nancy and we went to school with them and knew them very well and liked them. They both turned out a lot better than many other guys we knew. I have often wondered how much that stigma affected their lives. I suspect that the present acceptance of such mores still doesn't totally remove the stigma in the life of an illegitimate child. Is the child or is the parent illegitimate?

I remember one afternoon when the fourteen–year–old daughter of our cook became quite ill. She was so sick that my dad eventually loaded her in the car and drove her sixteen miles to the emergency room at the Lancaster hospital.

The next morning at breakfast Mother asked if the child was all right and what was the ailment.

The cook responded, "Lawdy mercy, Miss Strauss, weren't nothing wrong wid her, she was just pregnant." The cook thought single parenting was to be expected and she and her three daughters practiced it without the assistance of food stamps or child support from Uncle Sam, but with the support of my father because she was our cook. Back in those days the landowner took total responsibility for taking care of sickness on the farm.

There were always some puzzles hiding here and there around Van Wyck when I was a boy. One was a mysterious white man who came off and on over several years and stayed with a black woman who lived alone. He was thought to be a Yankee from New York, but I don't think even Dad, who knew all things, could figure out his background or whereabouts. Or maybe he knew all about him and didn't think I needed to know. Uncle Warner would have told me if I had thought to ask him.

I do not know why I would remember this. As children we sometimes tuck away and forget bits of information and then have it return, years later, and see it coupled with some mores, learned years later, and see the old bit of information anew, in the light of the knowledge of the adult. Then we say, if only I had thought to ask.

I remember only a few newspaper headlines from the years when I was growing up. One was in

1927, *Lindberg Flies the Atlantic*. I was ten years old that year, and I think this great event first sparked my interest in aviation that has continued to this day. Flying has always occupied a special niche for me, from my first ride with a barnstormer, to soloing, and finally to owning and flying my own airplanes.

My first flight was with a barnstormer in an open cockpit Stearman biplane. He was flying out of a farmer's field near Waxhaw. The air rushing by made me feel like we were going at an unbelievable high speed. Mr. Henry Collin's livery stable, sitting on the town square in Waxhaw, certainly looked different from the air.

The memory of my first flight has carried with it to this day the potential danger of flying. The barnstormer I had flown with shortened his stay that week and flew quickly away without even refueling when a young girl walked into the whirling propeller on his plane and was nearly killed.

My second chance to take a ride in a plane was in an amphibian. Uncle Webb White was the Shell Oil Company distributor in York County and Shell brought a plane to Rock Hill as a marketing promotion. City fathers and other prominent citizens, five or six at a time, were taken for free rides over the town, and on every third or fourth flight the pilot would land on Lake Wilie, taxi on the lake for several miles before taking off again and landing, on wheels this time, to take off with another load at the Rock Hill airport. I latched onto one of the water flights. It was a great ride in a closed cabin, twin–engine, retractible landing gear amphibious airplane. A formidable machine for its day.

The second headline I remember was in 1929, *The Stock Market Crashes*. Not that my family lost a fortune in stocks that day, or that I even realized the magnitude of the news. I was twelve years old at the time and totally absorbed with getting the cows milked and not missing the school bus on cold frosty mornings. But it wasn't long before shock waves from the crash were felt way out in the hinterlands and those of us who grew up during the resulting Depression will always carry the year 1929 engraved in our psyches.

The year 1929 stands out in my memory for another reason as well: that was the year that the Catawba River rose and covered our part of South Carolina with a ferocious flood we called the Big River. It was ironic that Dad was away from home the night the Big River came. I don't think he ever spent a dozen nights away from home for his entire married life, but when it rained for three days and three nights in the fall of 1929, he was eighty miles away in Greenwood, on Grand Jury duty.

We were just finishing breakfast before catching the bus and heading for school when Uncle Kudge came to the house and told Mother that the Catawba River had overflowed its banks and that water stretched a half–mile wide from hill to hill. The bottomland corn crop was covered. A herd of cattle that had been grazing in the bottomland pastures was marooned on a narrow stretch of high ground that had been transformed into an island far from the water's edge, and the water was still rising.

John Ed was away, too. Mother quickly corralled all the available farm hands for a rescue mission. Oliver and I hitched up the wagon and fetched a rowboat from our swimming pond near the house. The crew of six or eight climbed into the wagon on top of the boat, and the mules trotted off for the river, a mile away. We reached the edge of water 300 yards before reaching the normal river banks. The river boiled by, filled with planks and logs and brush, and, believe it or not, some bales of cotton. The fifty–odd stranded cows stood bawling fearfully on a narrow strip of land that was growing narrower by the moment, for the water continued to rise.

There was about 200 yards of surging river between us and the cows. Mother asked for two volunteers to row out and drive the cows off the island, hoping they would be able to swim to shore. A cow is not noted for its swimming ability. It is surprising to me that it can swim at all. I suppose the cow's big body and large stomach causes it to be buoyant enough to float and it moves forward by waggling its spindly legs.

In those days, it was unusual for our Negroes to know how to swim, so volunteers weren't forthcoming, despite Mother's inducement of five dollars. We were all very scared. Oliver and I were good swimmers, and we volunteered. Dan Massey, who could just stay afloat with a "dog paddle," also volunteered. The three of us climbed into our little row boat and paddled into the treacherous torrent. It was immediately apparent that the current was so fast that we couldn't possibly row against it to the high ground where the cows were.

We quickly paddled the boat back to the shore while drifting still further downstream. Then we estimated how far the boat would be swept downstream by the current while crossing to the island and we carried the boat that far upstream from where we originally started and put in again. Then, while rowing 200 yards or so across the swift river while being swept 200 yards rapidly down the stream, we were able to reach the island.

Mother's plan was for the people left on shore to call the cows while Oliver and Dan and I beat them on their stubby rear ends with our paddles and drove them off their dry haven on the island. The first cow, braver or more terrified than the others, finally waded into the swift current and set off swimming for shore. Another followed and another. The herd swam, fifty–odd cows strong.

Even though the current took them hundreds of yards down the river before they landed, most of them made it. Only five or six cows were swept away. The balance of the herd was saved.

We paddled back across behind the last cow, not caring how far we drifted downstream. Mother gave each of us the five dollars reward and we all congratulated ourselves on the heroic and successful rescue campaign.

When we reached home several hours later, we learned that Uncle Hurley, another of Dad's tenants, had drowned when the boat that he was rowing across the flooded Twelve Mile Creek to reach Van Wyck had capsized.

Still another incident that made the Big River so foreboding was the fact that Dad had lost his entire herd of cattle just a couple of years before to the hoof–and–mouth disease. This disease is so contagious that when one cow is afflicted the entire herd must be destroyed. It was a grievous event when we had to drive our herd of about forty cows into a deep gully on the back side of the farm and shoot them one by one. Then we hauled in several loads of firewood, built a bonfire and tended it for forty–eight hours to burn the dead cattle.

This was a major blow to my father, and is a great example of the risk that farmers bore in those days. They were repeatedly subjected to major financial losses from unexpected disasters. It also helps explain why so many were willing to accept emergency relief and farm subsidies from Uncle Sam beginning with the days of Roosevelt and the New Deal.

I remember one hot August afternoon when the whole family was swimming. It was during the week of the Bank Holiday called by F.D.R. soon after he became president. Dad had returned from Lancaster where he did his banking, and as he approached the swimming pond, he waved to Mother and said: "Charley Jones shot himself last night." Mother immediately asked, "Was it because of the bank?"

Charley Jones was president of the Bank of Lancaster, where Dad did business. Dad responded, "I feel sure it was not the bank." Mother and Dad were friends with the Jones family and Mrs. Jones was a distant relative. A few days later the local papers were filled with headline stories about Charley Jones. He had tried to save his faltering bank by risky speculation on Wall Street, no doubt in the derivative equivalents of those days.

As I remember the story, Dad had all his liquid cash in that bank, but since August was his low point in cash, he didn't lose a great deal. Eventually he received fifty cents on the dollar, but the bank never reopened.

The deluge of bank failures during the early 1930s made it easy for legislators to pass laws establishing the FDIC, the Federal Depositors Insurance Corporation, to "protect" depositors.

But Dad was one of those people who hated the New Deal. He believed strongly in self–reliance and personal responsibility, and he had no patience whatever with Roosevelt and his policies.

On these matters he had a staunch ally in one of Mother's favorite relatives, her uncle James Walker. He was a bachelor farmer and lived by the Pacolet River sixty or seventy miles west of Van Wyck near Greenwood. Uncle James and Dad were good friends. They had a lot in common: they were both farmers, they both hated F.D.R., and they were both convinced he was ruining the country with the New Deal.

At least twice a year, after crops were laid by and late in the winter when there was plenty of leisure time to talk, Uncle James would come and visit for two weeks. I remember the end of one of these visits, after Dad and Uncle James had spent days solving all the government problems. As Uncle James, at an age greater than three–score–and–ten, was getting in his car to leave, he said, while shaking Dad's hand, "Edwin, I only wish that I could live long enough to see how all this mess F.D.R. has caused comes out."

I think about that statement now, seventy years later. Some things never change, I guess.

Uncle James Walker still drove his Model T Ford at that time, whereas Dad had recently bought a new V–8 Model A. Oliver and I had gone to Fort Mill with Dad to pick up the new car. We were told by the owner of the Ford dealership that the car should not be driven more than thirty miles per hour for the first 1,000 miles. On the way home Dad started feeling quite frisky about his new car and he took it up to forty–five miles per hour. Oliver and I shouted at him to immediately reduce the speed or he would ruin the engine. He smiled with pleasure at our responsible attitudes and slowed it to thirty.

When we got home and put the car in the garage, Oliver and I stood for a long time with Mother and admired it. I remember Oliver saying, "Jim, I don't think we will ever have another car as beautiful as this new Ford." I agreed, and Mother said, "Yes, boys, it is a beautiful car."

It wasn't too long afterward that Uncle Jim bought his Packard with spare tires on the fenders and Uncle Grady bought a new Essex. Uncle Verner's Stanley Steamer, the car of all cars, had been decommissioned by this time.

I was at the age when boys love mechanical things, and I spent hours drawing pictures of cars that existed and neater cars that I thought should exist. My sister Nancy, who was sometimes prone to exaggerate, said I became so compulsive that I drew cars on the fly leaves of every book in the house. I also collected some clay from the banks of the Catawba and made automotive sculptures, with and without fenders.

While I was busy making imaginary cars, John Ed was a junior in college at Chapel Hill, gaining experience with the real world. One weekend he arrived home in what we called then a "strip–down" car. It was a Model T Ford chassis without a body of any kind. The driver sat on a board on top of the gas tank beneath the steering wheel with no fenders or windshield for protection.

During this visit, when John Ed got Oliver and me away from Mother, he told us in the strictest confidence about his trip home. When he stopped for gas on the way home, a stranger had pulled up beside him and said: "Young man, I have been following you for thirty miles. I know you don't have a speedometer, but I have been clocking you at forty miles per hour on the straightaway and forty–five downhill." We could not have been prouder of our big brother.

I don't think I incorporated John Ed's strip–down into any of my sketches because I was too busy trying to improve on my ideal, the Packard with its flowing fenders. The Model A Ford fenders were designed only to keep mud away and not to appeal to the public or a boy's fancy.

But long before fenders disappeared, the original Van Wyck "commuter," Sam Vaughan, appeared at church one Sunday in a brand new Pontiac, a new name in the General Motors lineup, between Chevrolet and Oldsmobile. That car, with the emblem of an Indian Chief on the hood, was just what Sam Vaughan needed to commute over an hour each way to his job as a clerk in the Men's Department at Ivey's Department Store in Charlotte.

The Vaughan family was prominent in Van Wyck. Sam's brother Robert spent his life working at the brickyard, and he and Jimmy Moore, who later became president of the Ashe Brick Company, were two lively young men about town, or the village anyway. Dad always tried to keep both of them at a few miles distance from my sister Nancy.

While Nancy was making her way through high school and I was approaching my own teen years, the Depression that followed the crash of 1929 was growing deeper and more serious. Every cent saved or earned became precious. In 1931, at the tender age of fourteen, I got a paying job driving the same school bus that I had worried about missing only a couple of years before.

No test was required. Mr. Sam Thompson was the trustee in charge of school transportation and Mr. Sam knew I was a dependable kid. He had seen me driving a lot with my dad. He had no reason to doubt that I could handle the job. This was several years before a driver's license was required in South Carolina.

This was also before the River Road in front of our house was paved so it was a slippery year, sliding into ditches, making kids behave. About halfway through the year, Lancaster County went bankrupt, and from then on I was paid in script, I.O.U.s with some indefinite future value. Dad cashed my script for fifty cents on the dollar, and this was the beginning of my education in the futures markets.

By this time, Mother had resumed teaching at Van Wyck. Despite her input, even after consolidating with other Lancaster County schools, the Van Wyck school still wasn't a shining light as an educational institution. By the time John Ed graduated from high school there were only two other students left in his class and John Ed was salutatorian. You can bet your life that his younger sisters and brothers teased him aplenty about that "honor".

Mother didn't think her Nisbet children were supposed to be salutatorians by default. So off went brother Oliver to board with Aunt Emma Lee White in Rock Hill to finish his senior year, back at the Winthop training school.

A year behind Oliver, I also returned to Rock Hill to board with Aunt Emma Lee. I wasn't too happy about it because I had just reached my stride at the Van Wyck school. I was especially sorry to leave so soon after the Junior/Senior prom.

Mother had loaned me her car for the occasion, and off I had gone to pick up Sara Hudson, my date for the prom. She lived on a farm about five miles away, down on Old Hickory road, toward the Old Waxhaw Church. Her dad was a farmer and a hunter, and he kept a pair of beagle hounds. The hounds greeted me with loud barking and mean growls, then began nipping at my heels. Sara hurried into the car and I quickly drove away. Pressed by the hounds, I neglected to make my manners with her parents.

After the party I drove her home, ever so slowly, under a full moon, holding her hand in anticipation of our first kiss. When we pulled into her driveway the dogs were waiting, in full force. They barked and growled and raised such a ruckus that lights went on in the house and Sara jumped out of the car and ran inside. Before she was well in the house, I drove rapidly away, fearing for my tires.

The next Monday, back in school, I told Sara about my disappointment in not getting a kiss. We arranged to be the last to leave the classroom that day and before I knew it, Sara planted a big kiss smack on my lips and we tarried there, touching. I was so excited I damn near jumped out the second story window.

And so it was that I was not very keen on the idea of boarding in Rock Hill for my senior year. But I managed to have a little fun. My most memorable experience of the entire year, oddly enough, involved another girl and another prom.

I also had the good fortune to make friends with the boy who took tickets at the local movie house and I saw all the movies that year for free. Some of the romantic scenes were unforgettable.

As the end of the term approached, I was feeling pretty tired of school and pretty sure of myself. A few days before graduation, I left Rock Hill early one Friday morning for a weekend at home and failed to turn in a final English term paper that was required for graduation. The teacher called Aunt Emma Lee on the phone and told her I would not graduate the following week. Aunt Emma Lee put her son in her car and sent him straight to Van Wyck to fetch me. When we got back to Rock Hill and to school on the following Saturday morning, I was boldly confronted by an irate teacher.

She sat me down and told me to write a theme of several pages about any subject I chose. I did, and she was so pleased she not only passed me but gave me a B on the paper. The subject was hogkilling time on the farm.

It had been an interesting year in Rock Hill. While I was there I had to develop a special system for transportation to get home on weekends. I learned there was a York County school bus that left the Rock Hill public school fifteen minutes after we got out of my school at Winthrop. It traveled southeast and crossed the Seaboard Railroad tracks six miles south of Van Wyck. On Friday afternoons when I wanted to go home, I would run the mile and a half from my school to the public school and climb aboard that bus for a lift to the Seaboard tracks. The driver would let me off there and I would walk the six miles to Van Wyck. The Catawba River bridge trestle had to be crossed a mile before reaching Van Wyck, and I would listen ever so carefully to be sure a distant train was not coming before I rapidly crossed the railroad bridge, stepping briskly from railway tie to tie while staring at the water between, thirty feet below. On the return trip on Sunday I hitched a ride with Mr. Brown, who returned to his home near Rock Hill after his sermon in the Van Wyck Presbyterian church, and after he had shared a hearty meal with a member of the church.

I graduated from high school in the spring of 1933, when I was sixteen years old. A few weeks later, on June 25, 1933, the following notice appeared on the obituary page of The Charlotte Observer:

> *Dr. James Douglas Nisbet died of heart failure at the Charlotte Memorial Hospital. He was 67. After retiring from his medical practice in New York City in 1923, he had lived on his 2,000–acre farm with his wife, Beulah Hayes Nisbet, in Van Wyck, South Carolina, 25*

miles south of Charlotte. Dr. Nisbet had no children. He is survived by his wife, Beulah, and two brothers, Dr. W. Olin Nisbet of Charlotte and Dr. Verner S. Nisbet of Philadelphia, and by 11 nieces and nephews. He was born in the Old Waxhaws area of South Carolina. He graduated from Davidson College and the Charleston Medical School. He did medical graduate work in Germany and was the author of learned papers and journals. In 1895 he published the medical text book, Diseases of the Stomach.

It was ironic that Uncle Jim died so soon after my graduation. As his namesake, I had always been singled out for special favors, like the new suit he bought me each year for Christmas. I never expected anything more from him, and so I was surprised by the magnanimous offer he had made two years before he died, to pay for my college education. But there was a string attached. He specified that *his* plan was for me to attend Duke University and study medicine. He didn't ask if I had any plans of my own, or if I had any interest in the field of medicine. Uncle Jim had set his mind that his namesake would carry forward his name as a medical doctor. Uncle Jim was accustomed to having his way.

At the time Dad already had three children in college, John, Nancy and Oliver, and two more about ready to go. Adding me and later Alice to the already burdensome college expenses would have been overwhelming. To have my college education paid for by someone else was a big factor in our household. But I don't remember an ounce of pressure from Dad for me to compromise my interest between medicine and engineering.

On a visit with Uncle Jim a couple of months before he died, I told him that I had applied to Clemson and planned to study engineering. He showed his displeasure by changing the subject.

I think Uncle Jim had harbored a suspicion for a long time that this namesake of his might not be up to his expectations, as they say, he might be just no–account. Maybe it was the week I spent with him a couple of years before he died. Every summer Aunt Beulah went to New York City for her annual shopping spree. Uncle Jim usually went along, but this time he didn't feel up to the trip, so Aunt Beulah asked me if I could spend the nights with him while she was away. She didn't want to leave him alone at night when the household servants were away (the cook, the maid, and the chauffeur who doubled as a butler). Of course I agreed. The pay was good, a dollar per night.

The breakfasts were even better. Breakfast began with shredded wheat with peaches, and cream so rich it could barely be poured from the pitcher. This was always followed with scrambled eggs, sausage and grits. Uncle Jim's medical textbook was about diseases of the stomach, not about smoking a pipe, nor weighing in at 200 pounds on his five–foot–five frame, nor about cholesterol, nor about the cardiac arrest that would later take his life.

The only drawback to the job was the awkwardness between us. How could a fourteen–year–old boy develop a rapport with an old man who wore a cutaway coat and striped pants to breakfast every morning when he was not going out as far as the mailbox that day?

During breakfast one morning while we carried on our usual halting and unnatural conversation, Uncle Jim asked, "Jim, did you hear the commotion last night?" Always in awe of the man, I answered, "No, Sir, I didn't hear a thing." "Well," he said, "there was a terrible noise in the chicken house last night, and I went out to investigate. Of course I took my shotgun along. Sure enough, there was a fox stealing the chickens. I blasted the fox with both barrels." He took another bite of sausage and added, "The noise from the shotgun must have carried far and wide because Selwyn (the chauffeur, who lived a quarter of a mile away) was awakened and hurried over to investigate. You do sleep well, Jim."

At this point, I was not sure that I could or should fulfill my commitment to continue and sleep there to "protect" Uncle Jim until Aunt Beulah returned.

On another occasion during the same summer, he offered me a dollar for every hawk I killed. I disappointed him again. I walked many miles that summer with my .410–gauge shotgun, but all the hawks I saw were flying higher than the range of my gun, and I failed to bag a single one.

When Uncle Jim had practiced medicine in New York City, he often vacationed by hunting and fishing in Canada. When he retired to his farm in South Carolina, he continued to do so. And his namesake couldn't even bag a hawk.

A few days after Uncle Jim's funeral, the relatives gathered to hear the reading of his will at Aunt Beulah's big house. There was much speculation behind the scenes as to whether Uncle Jim had bestowed any inheritance on his eleven nieces and nephews and twenty–five grand nieces and grand nephews.

After all the boiler plate that lawyers like to write in wills and any other papers they can get their hands on, and after bequeathing everything to Aunt Beulah during her lifetime, the will read as follows:

> SIXTH: *Upon the death of my said wife, I hereby direct that the following legacies shall be paid out of the said residue remaining undisposed of at said time.*

1. To my brother, Julius Marcellus Nisbet, of Van Wyck, South Carolina, the sum of ten thousand dollars ($10,000).

2. To my niece, Loma May Nisbet, of Charlotte North Carolina, the sum of five thousand dollars ($5000)

3. To my nephew, John Edwin Nisbet, of Van Wyck, South Carolina, the sum of five thousand dollars ($5000).

4. To my grand nephew and namesake, James Douglas Nisbet II, of Van Wyck, South Carolina, the sum of ten thousand dollars ($10,000).

There were a few audible oohs and aahs from the assembled relatives. And there were at least two great sighs of relief, from me and my father. The ten thousand dollars left to me would pay my way through Clemson with plenty to spare. I began to have fond memories of Uncle Jim. Then I remembered, with a start, that the first clause in the will had left everything to Aunt Beulah during her lifetime and she was a relatively young woman.

Everyone thought it was all over and done, but then the reading of a codicil to the will commenced:

I hereby revoke and cancel Item SIXTH of my said last will and testament, and each and every bequest therein.

I direct upon the death of my said wife, the residue of my estate remaining undisposed of shall be divided into four (4) equal portions and distributed per stirpes among my heirs.

New and louder ooohs and aaahs were heard, but from different voices. The windfalls to Uncle Jule, Aunt Loma, Dad and myself never enjoyed even a half–life and I was not very high on the list of "per stirpers."

This codicil revealed an interesting twist in the complex mind of Uncle Jim. In the case of Aunt Loma, the twist was a cruel one. Aunt Loma had devoted her youth, her formative years, and her courting years, when she might have been finding a husband, to the care of her grandmother, Uncle Jim's mother, the matriarch of the Nisbet clan who died soon after Uncle Jim retired to Van Wyck. Yet, having first honored her sacrifices with his bequest, he for some unfathomable reason decided to retract the gift. Five thousand dollars was only a small percentage of Uncle Jim's estate, yet it would have made an enormous difference in the life of Aunt Loma. She had become a schoolteacher in Charlotte when Uncle Jim retired to the Ivey place and she continued to teach and live there with her widowed sister, Aunt Evelyn, for the rest of her life.

My father was crushed. He thought he had an understanding with Uncle Jim that he would be taken care of if he devoted himself to the management of Uncle Jim's farms as well as his own. Dad certainly deserved something. He also

110

thought he had helped relieve the loneliness and boredom of our old uncle who had grown accustomed to and had now lost, like all doctors eventually lose, their lives of being kowtowed to and doted over and never being challenged by their loving and respectful patients.

For my part, I was both hurt and confused. My question was: How did I displease or anger Uncle Jim to such an extent that, having first flattered me with such a valuable gift, he would subsequently alter the will by codicil to cancel it? The codicil cutting me out had been signed on January 31, 1933. I remembered that the only time he visited me when I was staying in Rock Hill with Aunt Emma Lee was about mid–winter in 1933. Did something bad happen during that visit, or was he holding a grudge about the fox in the hen house? Why didn't he simply write a fresh will with such perfidious indignation omitted and keep the secret to himself?

Besides being dizzy from the speed at which ten thousand dollars had passed through my fingers, I was also in something of a panic. College was fast approaching. And the man who had offered to pay my tuition was dead.

There wasn't time to set aside a long period for Aunt Beulah to mourn the loss of her husband, because I was getting desperate for an answer about my potential scholarship. I knew I could never save enough driving a tractor to pay for college tuition.

So, soon after the funeral, I went to visit her. Her keys still dangled from a chain around her waist. She was very pleasant and we chatted about farm matters for a while, and she told me about the adjustments she would have to make and that she planned to hire a live–in caretaker for the house. Finally, I gathered my courage and asked: "Did the offer from Uncle Jim to pay for my education hinge on Duke and medicine and otherwise nothing? You know he covered a lot of ground in his will and in the codicil, but he didn't mention the scholarship either way."

I think Dad and I were equally relieved when I learned from Aunt Beulah that "Dr. Jim," as she always referred to him (except when she addressed him directly as "Douglas"), had always intended to pay for my college education, although he had expressed deep disappointment that I arbitrarily had chosen not to carry on the great Nisbet name that he had stamped on medicine.

Actually, I don't think Uncle Jim was the only person who was hoping I would go into medicine. We had doctors on both sides of our family and I think Mother especially would have been pleased to see me follow suit.

Mother's father was Dr. Miles Walker. He practiced for all of his life in York, South Carolina, traveling by horse and buggy to his patient's homes far out into the county and curing their ills with a very limited supply of medication but with a healthy and effective bedside manner. Mother often talked about the great adventures and a few sad times she had, while traveling with her father.

Another of Dr. Miles' claims to fame was the invention of Papa's Salve, which was generously dispensed by Mother to cure the festering boils that seemed to frequent the young ones in our household. Mother was also big on castor oil, a standby for children's ailments of any sort. The very thought of a dose of castor oil frequently staved off any mention of a headache or a sore throat or a belly ache.

Mother's uncle on her mother's side, George Walker, was also a doctor. (Both of Mother's parents shared the same last name, Walker). Uncle George practiced at Johns Hopkins in Baltimore all of his career. He died in the same year that Uncle Jim passed away. His death, shall I say, was also very exciting because he was a bachelor and was rumored to possess a small fortune. Mother and her three sisters were the only living heirs.

Our family and the families of Mother's three sisters all gathered with great expectations for the reading of this will. Dad didn't normally carry a smirk on his face, but on this occasion he did. I suppose he thought, with the utmost confidence, that after this will was probated he would not have to worry any more about small matters like the costs of college educations. After all, Mother was a twenty–five percent heir, a sure lock on Uncle George's estate that was estimated to be half a million dollars. The will was read:

I, Dr. George Walker, being of sound mind, do hereby bequeath $5,000 to my faithful housekeeper, and $10,000 to each of my beloved nieces, Alma Sharp, Strauss Nisbet, Mary Hollis, and Olive Hardin, along with all of my personal property.

The entire balance of my estate will be placed in a trust for cancer research under the direction of my friends and colleagues at Johns Hopkins School of Medicine.

So went the reading of the will of my third rich great–uncle.

Having secured the promise of a scholarship from Aunt Beulah, I set about enjoying my last summer before college.

My brother John Ed had already graduated. He had gone to Clemson for two years, then transferred to the University of North Carolina at Chapel Hill. There he majored in geology, a subject that well suited his interest in natural things like rocks, quail, rabbits, mink he trapped, and a showpiece collection of Indian arrowheads and tomahawks that he found on the land. Geology jobs were not too easy to come by in the middle of the

Depression, however, so he had taken a job teaching school. Therefore, having the summer off, he had decided to travel to Chicago to see the World's Fair. Five of his friends were going along, and when one of them canceled at the last minute, John Ed offered the extra spot to me. With an invitation like that I was sure I could float a loan from Mother to pay my way.

We left home for that great experience, six of us, three boys and three girls, in a Chrysler sedan that Dad had recently extended himself to buy, and in the middle of the Depression yet. In Chicago sleeping quarters were arranged for at the home of a relative of one of the girls. At other stops the oldest girl assumed the chaperone responsibilities.

I had never been west of Asheville, nor north of Greensboro, nor south of Columbia, not even to Myrtle Beach, so I was curious to see the lands beyond the Carolinas. The Chicago World's Fair was fascinating and I saw a bigger world than I had known before. I was particularly impressed by exhibits put on by General Motors and General Electric.

We returned via Toronto. Unlike the United States at that prehistoric time, Canada was a wet country, where liquor was sold and drinking was allowed. I am sure John Ed and the other older members of our tour had previous experience with liquor. They had all been away to college for several years, but it was my first affair with Canadian Club.

The Canadian Club soon opened my eyes to a fairyland and just as quickly closed my eyes to sleep and then opened them again to the worst hangover I have ever had.

Another highlight of that memorable trip was my first visit to New York City. In the two weeks we were traveling I got to know one of the older girls pretty well and hated to see the trip end.

By the time we got back to South Carolina, college was close at hand. Dad and Mother drove Oliver and me to Clemson, for Oliver to enter his sophomore year and for me to enter as a freshman. Clemson was a military school, and I had learned from Oliver that I would be issued a military uniform: two pairs of trousers, two shirts, a jacket with a Sam Brown belt, a cap and a mackinaw. So, besides what I wore, which was about all I owned, I had packed only underwear, socks, pajamas, a toothbrush and a razor. I was only sixteen years old and didn't need to shave but once a week, but I figured as time passed I would need the razor more often, maybe every day before I graduated.

On the three–hour drive from Van Wyck, I don't remember what we talked about, but I do remember that as we entered the city limits of the small town of Clemson, I could see the college, sitting in the foothills of the Blue Ridge Mountains in the far northeastern part of South Carolina. All the buildings were made of brick. A large four–story administration building in the center of the campus was surrounded by four three–story barracks for living quarters, a library, a YMCA, and several classroom buildings for engineering, textiles, agriculture, and chemistry.

As we pulled in to park at the administration building, Oliver said, "Jim, as soon as we stop in the parking lot, a couple of upperclassmen will greet us and ask you to step out of the car."

Then things started to happen fast.

Before Mother and Dad could get out to see what was going on, two boys had grabbed me and shaved my head. Then they said, "Welcome to Clemson, Rat Nisbet." I just stood there and watched as the barbers, or barbarians, walked away, laughing, waiting for the next car to pull in so they could create another "Rat."

Oliver, who had suffered the same treatment the year before, took me to the guard house to check me in and left me there. I was barely able to tell Mother and Dad goodbye before they were gone.

I was issued my room number and escorted to it by a military–type corporal, a fresh sophomore who had been selected to return early to help with freshman orientation. Another sophomore was waiting when I arrived at my room. He told me to lean forward in my doorway so that he could properly welcome me to the barracks. He stood in the wide hallway and took a sweeping swing with a broom and hit me with five hard blows on my butt. When he finished, he said, "Welcome to my barracks, rat. You are hereby assigned to clean my room."

The shaved head and the designation "rat" were designed to clearly identify freshmen as the lowest form of life. Freshmen served upperclassmen by cleaning their rooms, running their errands and generally satisfying their every whim.

I entered the room to find two more strangers inside, two roommates who had already moved in and had claimed the two bottom bunks. I felt like a jailbird: barracks, bunks, and being welcomed with a beating.

Before the second day ended, I learned more about this strange place where my parents had left me, and the ritual about which Oliver had not briefed me very well. Reveille at 6 a.m., pile out of bed, get dressed, stand in formation, answer to roll call, stand for inspection and march to breakfast with a corporal trying to make sergeant calling out the cadence, *one–two–three–four, one–two–three–four*. Repeat at noon: formation, roll call, stand for inspection and march to lunch, wasn't it supposed to be dinner? *One–two–three–four.* Repeat at 6: formation, roll call, stand for inspection and march to dinner, I always had called it supper, *one–two–three–four*. Then taps at 11 and inspection of the room to see that every head was safely accounted for and tucked in.

I remember thinking: I never had that much trouble finding my way out of bed and to meals and back to bed when I was at home, and right then, home was where I wanted to be. I would have preferred that Mother tuck me in, but my boyhood on the farm had ended.

After I had been at Clemson four or five weeks, I received a letter from Aunt Beulah, saying, "My old roommate from Goucher College, Ethyl Clyde, is visiting me and we will be motoring down to Florida soon. If you can get home this weekend, you can motor back to Clemson with us and we could see the Clemson Campus."

I got a pass for my first weekend leave and experienced my first of four years of hitchhiking home—that was the standard mode of transportation for Clemson Cadets.

After church and one of Mother's hearty Sunday dinners, Aunt Beulah and her friend Miss Ethyl Clyde arrived to pick me up for the trip back to Clemson. They were traveling in a Packard touring car. The top was down and there were two windshields, one for the front seat where the liveried chauffeur was sitting and another for the back seat where the smug Miss Clyde and a disoriented Aunt Beulah sat. Mother and Dad told us goodby and I climbed in with the chauffeur. The car turned a lot of heads as we drove through small mill towns on the way back to Clemson and when we arrived and were touring the campus it turned the heads of the Clemson cadets too. Word soon spread that some rat was riding around in a chauffeured Packard. We parked and I took my motoring companions for a walk around the parade grounds near the administration building. We stopped at the Soda–shop and I mischievously ordered a Coke and a moon pie for each of us. I knew a moon pie was not on the gourmet menu of the Clyde Steamship lines owned by Ethyl Clyde's parents, but it occurred to me that a moon pie would be good nourishment for the two ladies motoring to Florida.

When we returned to the car a crowd of cadets had gathered and the chauffeur was showing them the large trunk that sat strapped to the rear deck. It was filled with eight matching suitcases—for a frequent change of clothes in hot and sweaty Florida. The Chauffeur assisted Aunt Beulah and Ethyl Clyde into their seats and the three travelers motored on and I returned to my room to find a sophomore waiting to beat me with ten swats on my but, because rats are not supposed to ride in a chauffeured Packard.

I survived my freshman year as a rat, and tried to get used to marching in step. The only place on campus where you could buy a bar of candy or a Coke was the little shop in the back of the administration building. The well–known Frank Howard was the assistant football coach and his main source of recruits for the football team was freshmen he found while he hung out at the Jew Shop. The first day I passed the Jew Shop, Frank Howard stopped me, introduced himself and said, "You look like a big strong boy, why aren't you going out for football?" That is the way it was done in the old days before the stars were courted and recruited in high school. I had played football during my last year in high school and didn't like it very much and wasn't very good at it. Besides that, engineering students don't have time for college sports because their afternoons are filled with lab work.

At the end of my freshman year, I went back to Van Wyck and got a summer job working for John Ed, who had hired on with the U.S. Department of Agriculture as a soil conservation agent. The motto of the S.C.S. in those days was "To make the Catawba River run clear," and they were in the middle of one of F.D.R.'s big New Deal programs to terrace every field in the county.

John Ed gave me a job driving a caterpillar tractor that pulled the grader for terracing the land. The job paid forty cents an hour, but only when the tractor was in motion. It did not pay anything when the tractor was being repaired. Since the tractor was powered by a new diesel engine that had not been on the market long enough to be properly debugged, there were about as many down hours as driving hours.

When I got back to Clemson for my sophomore year, I took a course in woodworking. The course was interesting, but its instructor, Professor Marshall, was more interesting. A few years before my arrival, he had formed a flying club that had designed, built and flown a small single–engine airplane. This plane was suspended from the ceiling over the woodworking classroom for all subsequent students to see and admire and be distracted by.

The club that had accomplished that unusual feat was disbanded during the recession of 1930. Professor Marshall, upon learning of my fascination with airplanes, encouraged me to start a new flying club. He introduced me to a local army pilot who gave flying lessons in a two–seated, two–cylinder Aeronca that he flew from an abandoned golf course nearby.

Even back in the mid–1930s, flying lessons were expensive, so I wrote my most appealing letter to Aunt Beulah and asked if she would like to underwrite flying lessons as an important extracurricular activity for her favorite nephew and Uncle Jim's only namesake. She agreed to sponsor me, and with the help of the professor and the instructor, I organized and became president of a new Clemson flying club.

Last names were always used at Clemson. I remember the names of two of the eight or ten club members, a senior named Barney and a rat unforgettably named Lindbergh. Our instructor was the son of a local Methodist minister. He was also a drunk and was frequently tipsy when we flew with him. Believe it or not, the man often carried aboard a pint of white lightning and always ended his instruction period with a snap roll or two. We learned how to fly and soloed under this regime. In my many subsequent years of flying, I have owned eight airplanes and I remember a few close calls but very few that were as close as some of my early experiences with my first flying instructor.

Back then, the FAA had not developed many rules about flying. I was able to solo after only three hours of instructions. Now ten hours minimum is required. Now a student pilot must have a minimum of thirty–five hours before being eligible to be tested for a private license and only then can he take up passengers.

There was one time when our instructor gave me what might have been life–saving advice. I had planned to fly the Aeronca with my roommate home for a weekend. My instructor saw us off, and his last suggestion was that I circle the golf course several times and gain some altitude before departing off across the wooded forest that edged the course. I did, and as we completed the second 360–degree turn and I set the compass course to fly over the golf course and half of South Carolina, the engine failed.

Fortunately we had gained plenty of altitude and I circled back and landed on the golf course. Even though we finally stopped in a sand trap, it was better than in the middle of a tree.

None of our club projects would come close to the daring accomplishment of our predecessors who built the flyable small plane, but in addition to learning how to fly, we did have one other exciting project during my time in the flying club.

An Engineering Day was held each year at Clemson to illustrate feats of its engineers. For our project, Lindbergh, Barney and I moved an old twelve–cylinder World War I Liberty aircraft engine from its display and mounted it on a new stand outside the engineering building. Then we scraped together enough money to buy what we thought would be enough gas to last for four hours and fired it up.

The noise made by that monster was so great that everything else on the campus stopped until the president of the college shut us down.

Military Science and Tactics was a required course for all freshmen and sophomores at Clemson. After two years, students had an option to drop out of the courses, which I promptly did. I knew how to take a gun apart and put it back together before I ever went to Clemson.

But dropping out of ROTC did not allow me to rop out of all the other military rituals such as marching to meals and in parades on special days. I immediately became ineligible to be anything other than a private in the Cadet Corp, and I fell under the command and discipline of cadet corporals, sergeants, captains and colonels. Oliver, a year ahead of me, had risen through the ranks to Captain, but I considered all the military ritual a serious distraction to my progress in engineering.

During my last year at Clemson, I became more and more interested in my engineering courses and more and more rebellious of the military restraints. This recalcitrance reached a climax when I was called to the president's office. I had accumulated enough disciplinary demerits to be expelled. I remembered the often told family story about Uncle Taylor who was expelled from Clemson when he and two other cadets, one April fool night, actually put a cow in a classroom on the fourth floor of the administration building.

Up to this time I had seen President Sykes only at a distance when he was making speeches. When I was ushered into his office to be expelled, I had as my only hope a bit of inside information that I hoped would save the day.

Dr. Sykes rose from behind his big desk to greet me. He seemed like a pleasant fellow. "Have a seat, Nisbet," he said.

Before he could chastise me, I quickly launched my secret weapon. "Dr. Sykes, I understand you used to court my Aunt Jeannie Heath, before she married my uncle, Dr. Olin Nisbet. When I came to Clemson four years ago, Aunt Jeannie asked me to remind you of that fact if ever I had an occasion to meet you. I have been here four years but this is the first chance we've had to meet. It is my senior year, and I have only a month left before my graduation, sir."

We talked for ten more minutes about the latest whereabouts of Aunt Jeannie before getting back to the real subject at hand. Dr. Sykes said he would allow me to graduate. Looking back at the critical days just before graduating from both high school and college, I must say, I barely squeaked by.

Then, one spring morning in 1937, I was catapulted from college to a career. It was an exciting day for every senior in engineering at Clemson. A recruiting officer had arrived from General Electric to interview the engineering graduates. A job offer from G.E. was considered the top prize for an engineer. G.E. had a long–standing practice of recruiting at all the prominent engineering schools across the country—MIT, Stanford, Michigan, Rice, Georgia Tech—so an offer was a highly competitive business. Also, the Depression lingered on and we knew that G.E. was hiring fewer student engineers. The professors at Clemson said they would be pleased if only one or two graduates were hired by G.E. that year.

Head of the Engineering Recruiting Office at G.E. was a Mr. Borring. It was said that he hired more engineering graduates than any other man. I still have a vivid memory of Mr. Borring, a handsome, articulate fellow. He quickly developed a rapport with the engineering seniors during his lecture to them that morning. With a broad brush he painted a rosy picture of employment at G.E. He cited opportunities in many areas at that great company. Then he emphasized and elaborated on the Student Engineering Program which G.E. had developed over a long period of time. It was a post–graduate industry settling–in process leading to careers in engineering, sales or management. If we seniors had any doubts before, there were none now—a job with G.E. was the big prize.

I was fascinated with Mr. Borring's lecture about the largest conglomerate company in the world, whose name enjoyed the highest prestige in the industry. But I thought it was fruitless to sign up for a personal interview because G.E. had the reputation of hiring only top students of loftiest academic achievement. I had just missed Tau Beta Phi, which was the brand of excellence in engineering. A month earlier, I had gotten an appointment to the Naval Air Corps from the Senator of South Carolina, Jimmy Byrnes, who later became Governor of South Carolina and then Secretary of State under Truman. I had passed the

Navy's rigid physical exam and was all set and enthusiastic about going.

As I was leaving the lecture, Professor Fernow, the head of mechanical engineering, took me aside and told me to sign up for the interview. He said he had already spoken favorably on my behalf to Borring when he had reviewed the standing of Clemson engineers with him. This surprised and pleased me, so I signed up for an interview that afternoon. Fernow was the toughest professor at Clemson.

I suppose many of us, both during our formal education and later on, have experienced the profound and lasting influence of a great teacher. Fernow stands out in my mind as such a person. He was a gruff professor, cold, a rigid disciplinarian and a ruthless taskmaster. I was afraid of him, but I developed a tremendous respect for him.

Once when I passed Professor Fernow on campus and spoke to him with a self–conscious grin on my face, he stopped and gazed at me with a cold stare and asked, "What are you thinking about, Nisbet?" "Nothing," I said. Then he launched into an abrasive lecture about the stupidity of students who waste their time, wandering across campus to and from classes with blank minds when they could use that time for constructive thinking. He walked away saying: "Everybody is born equal in that each person has allotted to him twenty–four hours a day and I strongly suggest to you, Nisbet, that you start today to utilize your twenty–four hours a day rather than walk aimlessly across campus without a thought in your head and with only that silly grin on your face."

Now, years later, I vividly remember Fernow and that campus admonition. On many occasions since I have thought: "I must get my thinking done before this hour passes and sets me behind."

I thought I was hopelessly lost with Fernow although I worked harder under his stern stick than for any other professor. Then I was completely surprised in my senior year when he called me into his office and said he wanted me to be his lab assistant. I was to start at three o'clock that afternoon. Although I continued to be afraid of Fernow, I learned in working closely with him that under his crusty armor he was gentle and almost friendly at times. And now Fernow was my sponsor, recommending me to G.E.

Back in my room where several fellow students were having a bull session, I announced that I had a date with the G.E. recruiter and I would stroll down and get the prize job. My friends laughed aloud. One suggested that I change pants because the pair I had on had a hole in the knee and the pockets were frayed. I said my only other pair was even worse, and off I went with apprehension.

Professor Fernow introduced me to Borring and left the room. Before sitting down I said to Mr. Borring, "I understand you hire only the top students and I'm not the top nor the bottom either." He smiled and told me to have a seat. He said that I was the last on his list to be interviewed and he had plenty of time to chat. Half an hour later, to my pleased astonishment, I was offered a job at G.E.

When I announced this back in the barracks, my friends laughed heartily and didn't believe it, because a couple of them also had had interviews earlier and had been told that they would hear later.

The next morning as we were waiting for classes to begin, Fernow came by and congratulated me on getting an offer. My friends were aghast with disbelief. It turned out that I was the only one to receive an offer during the interview. Two others were notified later. I like to think that I was the only student that Fernow recommended. This was completely unexpected and an exhilarating experience. I also learned the importance of having a sponsor like Professor Fernow. I have observed many times in the years since that the men who move ahead in industry, as well as in preaching the Gospel, are often sponsored by those in high places—professors, elders and vice presidents.

Now I faced a decision: accept my appointment in the Naval Air Corps, or go to work for G.E. as a student engineer. The Air Corps would allow me to pursue my love of flying, but the G.E. job seemed to be a greater challenge and opportunity for a better career.

I graduated a month later and spent two restless weeks at home practicing typing by the touch method. It seemed like a worthwhile filler when I had nothing else to do and knew I would be writing letters home to Mother after I left and I wanted her to be able to read them. I have used it ever since. Before I left home, I traded my twelve–gauge shotgun to Oliver for his portable typewriter. That was the same gun that Uncle Jim had used to kill the fox.

I discussed the G.E. job offer and the Naval Air Corps appointment with Dad. The decision was already settled in my mind and I'm sure Dad knew it when he said, "Jim, I would suggest that you accept the student engineering program at G.E. In a year or two, if you still want to go to the Naval Air Corps, you can and you will have a broader engineering education that will be of great future value in anything else you want to undertake."

I said, "O.K., Dad, that settles it, but I don't have the money to get to Schenectady." Dad figured since I had graduated I was on my own. I argued that since I was only twenty I still had a year to go before I reached adulthood. He took me to the bank in Waxhaw, and the president of the bank, Mr. Jessie Williams, gladly loaned me $100 on a ninety–day note as soon as he learned Dad would cosign the note.

I didn't realize at the time that paying off the note at the rate of $30 per month from my $112 per month G.E. paycheck would be such a burden. I failed to take into account that I had to completely replace my Clemson military wardrobe with "civil" clothes and for the first time in my life I had to pay for my board and buy my own food. On top of this, insurance salesmen seemed to have the names of all student engineers before they arrived at Schenectady and they told convincing stories about the hazards of our jobs. I remembered that even tenant farmers back home had burial insurance, so I bought both life and accident policies and paid in advance from my dwindling cash.

When I was struggling to come up with the last payment on the note to the Bank in Waxhaw, I remembered my reserve source of funds. The year after Uncle Jim died, Aunt Beulah gave me the shotgun I had traded for the typewriter. She also gave me his big two-pound gold watch, with J.D.N. engraved on the back and with a gold face protecting the crystal. A fourteen-inch long, eighteen-carat gold chain came with it. I am ashamed to say I decided to pawn the watch. I am even more ashamed to admit that I didn't retrieve the watch but let it go for want of a ten dollar bill to redeem it.

A few days after the visit to the bank, Dad drove me to Charlotte and put me on the train to Philadelphia where Uncle Verner and Aunt Emma and Jack lived. I stopped off there to spend a long weekend with them on my way to my new job at G.E.

Aunt Emma was the most alert and astute lady I ever knew. When she learned that I was on my way to Schenectady, she found a friend who had a friend who knew a friend whose son was traveling by car from Philadelphia to Schenectady to go to work for G.E. She arranged for me to hitch a ride with him. He had to be the only guy in the state of Pennsylvania making that particular trip on that particular day to go to work for that particular company. Some people say, "It's a small world." Other people say, "We just travel in small circles."

My boyhood ended when I told my dad goodby and climbed aboard the train in Charlotte and left the South. My manhood began on Monday morning, June 21, 1937, when I walked down State Street and turned left on Erie Boulevard and continued walking toward a huge lighted G.E. monogram on top of building #2 in Schenectady, New York, and reported for work at the great General Electric Company.

For the next twenty years, first for sixteen years at G.E. and then at Cyclops, I worked on the cutting edge of science and modern technology, learning about and experimenting with materials for the construction of gas turbine engines for jet aircraft. In 1957, I decided to start my own business for the production of vacuum–melted alloys, which are essential for the efficient operation of gas turbines. I chose to locate my production plant back in the South, close to my roots, in the town of Monroe, North Carolina—a short twenty miles up the old Seaboard tracks from Van Wyck.

Much had changed in the twenty years since I left home. Dad had died in 1944 and Mother lived alone. When Oliver returned from the war, he lived with her off and on for several years. Then he was married and his wife Ida moved in. Oliver bought the house and land from Mother and he and Ida lived and raised their family at the old home place.

Oliver farmed a little, and in the springtime, representing a Charleston company, he sold fertilizer to farm stores across the state. In the fall he operated a cotton gin and bought and sold cotton. He spent a great deal of time preparing the Sunday school lessons that he taught in the adult class of the Presbyterian church. He liked the role of a gentleman farmer, and in keeping with that he was reluctant to remove the dozen or so outbuildings that in the past had been a necessary part of the operating farm. As they wasted away, a little ahead of their collapse, one by one, he tore down the horse barn, the corn crib, the hog barn, and four of the tenant houses. He converted the grainary into a house for his four boys where they lived and grew long hair to suit the style of the times.

When I returned to my roots at age forty to build a plant nearby, Oliver surprised and pleased me by offering to join me in that risky venture, risky indeed for two men in their early forties. Oliver was a natural salesman, a first class "people person." He complemented my technical and innovative business "bents" and we, with the help of many Union County farm boys, formed the nucleus for a great company.

Sadly, I was not able to renew my relationship with my older sister Nancy. She had also lived with Mother off and on while she alternated between teaching school and trying to overcome the tuberculosis that had plagued her for years. Nancy married Ted Moore when he returned from the war and they remodeled Mother's old four–room school house next to Miss Massey's boarding house. Ravaged by her disease, Nancy committed suicide in 1950 after the birth of her second son.

Mother lived for two years at Ted's, where she took care of Nancy's two baby boys, Taylor and Edwin Moore. When Ted remarried, she moved in with John Ed, still a bachelor who worked for the Department of Agriculture and lived on his farm in the same house where Dad was raised, three miles from our old home place.

Ten years later, when John Ed was fifty–five years old, he surprised himself and everyone one else by deciding to get married. One of his bachelor friends told him, "John, since you waited this long, looks like you could have waited it out."

A week before the wedding, another of his married friends who was a well–known practical joker advertised all of John Ed's hunting and fishing equipment for sale in the local paper with John Ed's phone number. A constantly ringing phone kept his mind off the wedding for several days.

When John Ed was married, Mother moved for the third and last time into a nice small house in the middle of Van Wyck that John Ed bought for her. Mother liked the house very much, but she never turned on the air conditioning. She liked her air to be natural and at the temperature that the Lord decided for it to be.

John Ed died from brain cancer in 1970, and Mother passed away in 1971 after falling out with her preacher because he couldn't tell her, to her satisfaction, what to expect in heaven.

Mother always said she did not want Van Wyck to change. In many ways I guess she got her wish. But in many other ways Van Wyck has changed a great deal.

South Carolina #1, the water tower that stood between the Seaboard tracks and Twelve Mile Creek, rotted away. Steam Locomotives were replaced with diesel engines which didn't need frequent watering.

The brickyard is still at Van Wyck, but rather than being hand–stoked with coal from West Virginia, automatic kilns are fired with natural gas piped in from Texas. The labor is still black and still paid the minimum wage. Red clay is hauled in from Indian Land township and blended with the sticky blue clay scooped up from the bottomland on Twelve Mile Creek and now bricks are made in any color including black. They *automatically* pass from the extrusion presses through the kilns and into the storage yard. The palettes of bricks are loaded on big heavy trucks which pass my old home place at seventy miles an hour on the way to brick veneer the new developments surrounding Charlotte's latest urban sprawl.

The five acres where I had my cotton patch is now growing forty–foot pine trees. The twenty acres where John Ed had his peach orchard has a good stand of winter oats. About the only farming left in the area is growing pine trees for pulp wood, the raw material for the only new industry that has landed near Van Wyck since the brickyard opened a hundred years ago. An English paper company called Bowater built a paper mill across the Catawba River to manufacture newsprint for the London Times. The pulpwood price is right cheap because the pine trees are subsidized by Uncle Sam.

All of the first five stores that originally opened in Van Wyck are gone. The only new store that was opened in recent years is now closed. The building that the last store was in still houses the U. S. Post Office, but the owner, Pete Yoder, the son of Mr. Cecil, broke with tradition and didn't become Postmaster. Not much mail is posted either in or out now, but I doubt if the Post Office will ever close. Let the federal budget be balanced some other place.

A few miles away, near the Catawba Bowater plant entrance where pulpwood truck traffic is constant, a new store called "Fast Bucks" was opened by Jimmy and Bobby Moore, the heirs to the brickyard property.

The tennis courts at Uncle Jim's Community Club House have grown up in trees. The club building, which used to be my great grandfather's home, sits silently, rotting away off Van Wyck road. The Van Wyck Community Club has been resurrected in a different place, above the volunteer fire house on top of the hill where the schoolhouse used to be.

The Van Wyck Presbyterian Church has grown back to perhaps 100 members. The congregation was cut in half in 1972 when one of the brothers, groping for something to talk about on a sunny spring morning after service, asked another if he believed in the direct words of the Bible. The second brother, thinking the conversation was the usual casual Sunday morning repartee, answered: "Well I guess I don't really believe in the direct words of the Bible in all its teaching." That would sound like a simple answer to a simple question, but it caused a rift in the Van Wyck Presbyterian church the likes of which had never been seen before or since.

Believers in the direct word formed against nonbelievers in the direct word and before the dust settled, two armed camps formed and the nice friendly little Van Wyck Presbyterian Church broke in two forever. The rift set the Alexander brothers against each other, and it set our sister–in–law Nezzie against Oliver's side as soon as she found out for sure where Oliver stood. Oliver and the doubters, after a court battle, held onto the property and the believers left. After holding service for four years in Sheron Thompson's abandoned store, the believers built a new building a couple of miles away.

Over the years, Oliver and I spent many hours talking about these changes and what we thought they portended. We didn't always agree on what was happening to our hometown, but that was nothing new. Oliver had been happy to spend his years planted at the old homestead, whereas I had wandered away.

After my wife Margy and I moved to Florida in 1987, we didn't see as much of Oliver and Ida as we had in the years before. We did visit with them at least twice a year when we migrated to and from our summer place in Rhode Island, and we were in frequent touch by telephone. It was in a telephone conversation with Oliver in the late summer of 1994 that he told me about his concern over Ida's recent loss of weight. I was doubly concerned, because I realized from our conversation that Oliver was not himself; his conversation was faltering and wandered far afield.

Two weeks later, Oliver was diagnosed with inoperable cancer of the brain and Ida was diagnosed with lung cancer.

Oliver died a few months later, on October 17, 1994. It was the same time of the year that Dad died, in the fall, after the farmers had gathered their crops. At Oliver's funeral, I sat in the old Presbyterian Church and looked up at the big solid walnut arch that Oliver had handcrafted and erected behind the pulpit many years before. During our childhood that walnut tree had stood like a sentinel by the side porch in our yard producing rich black walnuts.

I was calm, under a curious control of my emotions. The wake, the time to keep watch over a body until burial, is a ceremony evolved over eons of time, that creates an atmosphere that has a hypnotic effect on loved ones that literally, temporarily, shuts down normal emotions and bereavement for several days.

After the funeral service, the host of relatives and friends all gathered at "Oliver's Lodge" which he had built years before on a little pond near the

Catawba. Some of the timbers had come from our old cow barn and from an old wooden–geared cotton gin, and Oliver had salvaged others from various outbuildings around the countryside. It was a place built for entertaining, a place where Oliver could satisfy his love of people and his love of storytelling, where he could share his generous and gregarious personality by hosting business and family friends with fabulous pig roasts and simple family affairs. In the yard Oliver had mounted an unusually large bell made of the space metal Titanium. I had a sudden, strange, yet cheerful urge to strike the bell in memory of our lives together. I did, and I had forgotten how loud it was. I am sure Chief Blue and all the Indians on the Catawba reservation across the river heard the timbre of the tone and knew we were assembled at Oliver's Lodge.

Hours later I was still in a hypnotic state as Margy and I drove down the long lane back to Oliver's house, past the old fields and landmarks I knew so well. Then as we turned out of the driveway away from my old home place, the ceremonies that had shielded me, left me, and I could no longer hold back my emotions. I broke down and wept with grief over my brother, the latest person to be laid to rest at the Old Waxhaw Cemetery.

Ida lived alone at the old home place and appeared to be recuperating from her illness. Then in the spring of 1995, I heard she was again under chemotherapy treatment for both chest and lung cancer.

I wanted to see and visit and talk with Ida. I had heard that she and Nancy Crockett, who is in charge of the Old Waxhaw Cemetery, were debating about removing a huge thirty–foot cedar tree that had grown up in the middle of the Nisbet plot and was tilting aside the flat markers of John Ed and Nancy. I thought it would be nice if Ida and Nancy Crockett and I could go to the cemetery together, visit Oliver's grave, and see about the cedar tree.

When I called her to see if it suited her for me to call, she said, "I would like to see you Jim, but you must remember, I have good and bad days."

I took an early morning flight from Naples to Charlotte, rented a car, and drove straight to our old home place. It was a beautiful spring morning and I saw again that there is no prettier city in the world than Charlotte in the springtime, when the dogwoods, the flowering pears, the azaleas, rhododendron and jonquils are in full flower.

Ida had had a bad night and was having a bad day. She said she had been unable to get Nancy Crockett to join us and she was sorry, but didn't feel up to visiting the cemetery with me.

I spent only fifteen or twenty minutes with her. When I left, I walked alone, deep into the woods, beyond where Huss Barber's old tenant house had been. I kept on going, looking for Mother's favorite wildflower, yellow lady's slippers. Mother could always find them hiding in the ferns by the cool, moist, moss–covered banks of a stream. I saw only jack–in–the–pulpits preaching under a green canopy. I must have been too late for trillium, the very first sign of spring. The branch, fresh from spring rains, raced by, headed for Twelve Mile Creek, and on to the Catawba River, and on to join up with the Congaree and the Santee Cooper Rivers before reaching the sea.

I continued my walk to the Catawba River bottoms and saw a beaver dam on a branch just before it entered the river and fresh corn sprouting in the river bottoms where the Big River had flooded the land sixty odd years before. My mind reflected on the memory of Mother and fifty cows swimming for shore.

When I returned to the house, Caroline, Ida's daughter, was there and said Ida was sleeping. I left and headed for the Old Waxhaw Cemetery, alone.

When I passed through Van Wyck, I could not believe my eyes: There was a new sign on the old store building which had been Sheron Thompson's store and before that, almost a hundred years ago, had been Dad's store. The sign read, GUN SHOP.

I stopped and went in and foolishly asked the clerk who was tending the store: "Did you know my father used to own this place?" The clerk was a little startled and he said, "He don't no more."

I asked him about the dozens of assault weapons that were displayed on the wall behind a counter that was filled with pistols. He said, "The new gun law applied only to the sale of assault weapons manufactured after the law was passed. In anticipation of the law, the manufacturers had built and stored in warehouses around the world enough inventory of assault weapons to last us for ten years."

Depressed, I left the village, and drove on, wondering what kind of fruit would grow from this new seed planted at my dad's old store in Van Wyck. Surely the school boys loafing around the sidewalk and going into the Gun Shop to inspect the pistols and rifles and shotguns would be subjected to a much different influence than when I was a boy and went into Sheron Thompson's store to buy a Coke. On the other hand, when I was boy, I owned two shotguns, a rifle and a pistol, too.

When I reached the Old Waxhaw Cemetery, I realized that I had missed the chance to tell Ida and Nancy Crockett the real story about the cedar tree that had found a rich life in the middle of the Nisbet plot. I know the story is true because it was Mother's way. On the night after Mother was buried, she sent a spirit out from her body to scratch in the fresh soil over her grave to plant a seed for a cedar tree, to beautify the cemetery.

I stood by her cedar tree and revered the place where Daddy, Mother, little Miles, John Ed, Nancy, Kay (the mother of my four children), and recently my brother Oliver have quietly gone to take up eternal residence. Someday I will join them there.

Whether or not we will all meet at some heavenly place in the hereafter I do not know. But I do know, I will remember into eternity, the days when we were all at home together on the farm in Van Wyck, when I was a boy.

To Mother on Mother's day 1932
By Nancy Nisbet, 1914–1950

I awoke from a dream of childhood
And found you standing there
With your eyes smiling,
And the March winds in your hair.

I awoke from pain and heartache
And found you by my side
And I knew you had suffered with me,
By the tears you could not hide.

I awoke from a dream of happiness,
And found you happy too,
With the blue in the depth of your eyes,
Reflecting the dear joy, I knew.

And at my last awakening
It is my prayer,
That I will awake,
To find you waiting there.

ABOUT THE AUTHOR

James D. Nisbet grew up in Lancaster County, South Carolina, and attended Clemson College during the Great Depression. He graduated in 1937 with a B.S. degree in mechanical engineering and a lifelong interest in the pleasures and mechanics of flying. During World War II he developed a process for making materials for gas turbines in General Electric's research laboratory. In 1957 he founded Allvac Metals Company in Monroe, North Carolina, using vacuum–melting technology to produce high–temperature alloys. Since 1970 he has been a venture capitalist, money manager, stock market researcher, and author, publishing four books that cover the range of his working experience. He lives with his wife Margy, wintering in Naples, Florida and summering in Weekapaug, Rhode Island.

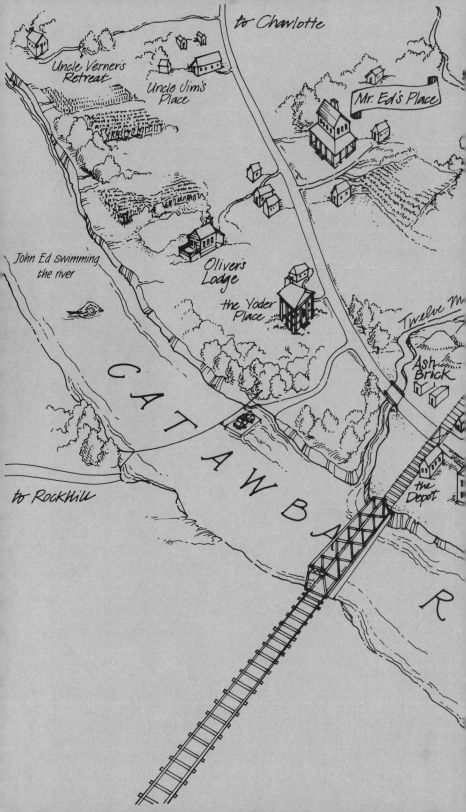